Praise for *Make Your Money Last a Lifetime*

"This little book contains some very useful information on how to successfully plan for and navigate the financial issues of one's retirement. I learned a lot from it."

> —Jack Canfield, Co-author of *Chicken Soup for the Soul®* book series

"Simply written, easily read, and spot-on with great advice for all of us in our golden years. If only one idea out of this book hits home for you, it'll be a home run."

> —David Allen International best-selling author of *Getting Things Done: The Art of Stress-Free Productivity*

"If you are serious about making your money last a lifetime, invest some time reading this delightful book. From sensible sustainable withdrawal rates to the power of investment policy statements to protecting yourself from identity theft... Kevin Bourke hits on all the critical financial skills for a fruitful retirement. Lest you think you don't have time—or wouldn't be interested—in such topics, guess again. A fun, quick read, this book is full of short stories and eye-opening anecdotes that make these vital financial concepts come alive."

> —Manisha Thakor, Co-author of *On My Own Two Feet* and *Get Financially Naked*

"This book is well written, easy to understand, and helpful for anyone facing retirement. It is a great book for adult children and seniors who may be facing many financial decisions as they age. As Kevin points out you do want to Make Your Money Last a Lifetime and Kevin can show you how!"

—Vickie Dellaquila, CPO, Author of *Don't Toss My Memories in the Trash: A Step-by-Step Guide to Helping Seniors Downsize, Organize, and Move*

"Bravo, Mr. Bourke, for creating easy and understandable explanations of investment choices for those of us who are afraid of outliving our money. Thank you for simplifying an intimidating subject so that we laymen could know where to protect and grow our hard-earned money. I love your use of examples and conversational writing style. Well done!"

—Susan Levine, MLS, the information Tamer for boomers and seniors and the Founder of 50somethinginfo.com

"This book turned my investing up-side-down... for the better. I was able to understand everything. AND that is a first for me and money matters! I'm planning to send it to all my "golden-age" friends to help them gild their investments."

—Rev. Dr. Sylvia Casberg, author and publisher, Sunny Fields Publishing

MAKE YOUR

MONEY

LAST A

LIFETIME

KEVIN

BOURKE

CERTIFIED FINANCIAL PLANNER CFP®
CHARTERED FINANCIAL CONSULTANT CHFC
CERTIFIED DIVORCE FINANCIAL ANALYST CDFA

ISBN-10: 0984789529

ISBN-13: 978-0-9847895-2-8

The scenarios presented in this book are for educational purposes only. Your results will vary.

Securities and advisory services offered through LPL Financial, a Registered Investment Advisor, Member FINRA/SIPC

This information is not intended to be a substitute for specific individualized tax or legal advice. We suggest that you discuss your specific situation with a qualified tax or legal advisor.

The opinions voiced in this material are for general information only and are not intended to provide specific advice or recommendations for any individual. To determine which investment(s) may be appropriate for you, consult your financial advisor prior to investing. All performance referenced is historical and is no guarantee of future results. All indices are unmanaged and cannot be invested into directly.

Asset Allocation does not ensure a profit or protect against a loss.

There is no guarantee that a diversified portfolio will enhance overall returns or outperform a non-diversified portfolio. Diversification does not ensure against market risk.

Government bonds and Treasury Bills are guaranteed by the US government as to the timely payment of principal and interest and, if held to maturity, offer a fixed rate of return and fixed principal value.

Stock investing involves risk including loss of principal.

Bonds are subject to market and interest rate risk if sold prior to maturity. Bond values and yields will decline as interest rates rise and bonds are subject to availability and change in price.

Investing in Real Estate Investment Trusts (REITS) involves special risks such as potential illiquidity and may not be suitable for all investors. There is no assurance that the investment objectives of this program will be attained.

Municipal bonds are subject to availability and change in price. They are subject to market and interest rate risk if sold prior to maturity. Bond values will decline as interest rates rise. Interest income may be subject to the alternative minimum tax. Municipal bonds are Federally tax-free but other state and local taxes may apply.

ACKNOWLEDGEMENTS

Thanks go to those who helped me finish this project:

Sylvia Casberg, Stephen Duneier, Michael Keenan, Susan Levine, Lynda Kurtzer and Marcia Meier for their ongoing editing, support and ideas.

Olivia and Rachael, for giving up some of their Dad's time and attention while he wrote, wrote, wrote.

And Diane for providing the inspiration to actually complete this book.

FOREWORD

Finance, while it interests me, is not my specialty. I founded a staffing company in 1979 that eventually sold to a privately held personnel company in 2006. That combined company made additional acquisitions and grew to over one billion dollars in annual sales. Because women's issues are important to me, I have been very active in the National Association of Women Business Owners, founded the International Women's Festivals and co-wrote a book called *Life Moments for Women.*

Entrepreneurship I know. Women's issues I'm passionate about. Investment management? For the most part I leave that to the experts.

So when Kevin Bourke asked me to read the manuscript for *Make Your Money Last a Lifetime* I thought it would be interesting, but I wasn't prepared for how much fun I would have reading it.

Nor did I expect to learn so much about investing so quickly and effortlessly.

After the first few pages, I was hooked. Kevin uses humor, short stories and analogies to make complex financial topics accessible to anyone. He's a gifted writer who delivers his message with clarity and ease of understanding.

In the ever-changing world of finance, it becomes increasingly important to find a firm footing. In this book, *Make Your Money Last a Lifetime,* Kevin Bourke has taken the mystery out of investing.

10,000 people retire every day in the United States and this will continue for many years. On average each of these individuals can expect to spend eighteen years in retirement. They are each rightfully concerned about making their money last a lifetime.

This adds up to the need for sound financial advice, which this book provides.

Some of the topics I especially enjoyed include "How to invest like a billionaire." Really? I always thought investing like a large institution was out of the reach of individual investors. In this chapter I learned differently.

Should we help our children financially? This question has arisen more frequently as our sluggish economy causes more adult children to look to their parents for help. Kevin addresses this in a way that gives us as parents permission to make a decision that's in everyone's best interests.

These are just a few of the helpful topics addressed.

As mentioned, women's issues are first and foremost

on my mind, and the statistics are worrisome. Poverty rates among women are about double those of men in all age categories. This can happen even to those who were affluent at one time. Also, according to the Government Accounting Office, the poverty rate among retirees is substantially higher for women than men.

While this book isn't aimed specifically toward women, the way it's written as well as the topics it covers can be a huge benefit to them. With assistance from this book, everyone, male and female, will be better prepared to 'make their money last a lifetime.'

With warm wishes for your success,

—Patty DeDominic

INTRODUCTION

Gloria paid over $100,000 in taxes in one year. Unnecessarily.

June, who is 78, watched as her investment portfolio dropped in value by 50 percent. After being independent her entire life, June had to move in with one of her children.

Pete and Olivia, both in their seventies, watched as their investments became worthless. At the same time their pension income was reduced by seventy-five percent.

Jim nearly sent $3,000 to his grandson who needed help. Just before sending the money, Jim learned that he was actually sending it to a con artist posing as his grandson.

Bill didn't intend to disinherit his only daughter, he just got busy and never filled out the proper paperwork.

Lorraine tried to do the right thing by saving a little money so she saved one half of one percent annually on her investments by comparing fees but gave up 55 percent of her principal because she didn't know some basic tax rules.

Unfortunately there is no end of true stories of retirees and seniors who have made big, unintentional mistakes with their finances. What they were doing seemed to make sense at the time, but in the end they came to grief financially.

For decades I've been helping investors make wise financial decisions. Along the way, I've heard countless sad tales from retirees, as well as their children, attorneys and tax preparers. I care deeply about these people and was impelled to write this book with the hope of making a difference. My mission is to help seniors, retirees and their adult children become smarter with their money.

For the most part I manage investments, but there are many important financial issues retirees face that need to be addressed, not all of them directly investment-related.

While we can't possibly answer every financial question in depth, you'll get a good start from reading this book. It's designed to give you a reference point for many of the questions you're likely to confront. Through the use of real life stories, you'll see some simple steps you can take to find your way to a worry-free retirement.

I'd love if all of us, including retirees and seniors, could focus on what makes us happy and live our lives without worry about money. That is the point of this book.

—Kevin Bourke

TABLE OF CONTENTS

Chapter 1

SHOULD I HELP MY KIDS?

When I was six years old, I was expendable. The lady in charge said so.

We were on United Airlines flying from Los Angeles to Detroit to visit my grandparents, aunts, uncles and the rest of the family clan. The flight seemed to take forever. We were sitting in the last row near the lavatories because my mom had read somewhere that this was the safest place to sit in the event of a crash.

I just thought it smelled.

"In the event of an emergency, oxygen masks will drop from the ceiling above your head." As she said it, the flight attendant—known as a "stewardess" in those days—held a sample oxygen mask in her hands and placed it over her head.

"First, place the mask over your own face, like so." On went the mask. "Then grasp the white cord, pulling firmly until you feel the rush of oxygen through the mask.

"Next, after your mask is safely and securely in place, help your children with their masks, repeating the process for them."

Let me get this straight: the plane is plummeting to Earth at four hundred miles per hour and my mom is going to be able to find her mask, put it on, pull the white cord and *then* put my mask on? By the time she was able to do that, we'd all be dead!

Clearly, children were at the bottom of the pecking order.

What made no sense then makes perfect sense now. As an adult, I now understand the logic behind the "place the oxygen mask on your face first, then help your children" concept. If the parents are unconscious, they will be in no position to help anyone with anything.

How does this relate to money? We all want to help our children, no matter their age, and you may have noticed that as our children get older, the help they need comes in ever larger dollar figures. You first feel it when your offspring gets a driver's license and wants a car. It only gets more expensive from there. When they're adults, the next thing they need help with is the purchase of a home. Our natural inclination is to help our children first, then take care of ourselves.

Recently a new client, Rachel, was sitting in my office, telling me she planned on helping her adult son and his family to purchase a house. While most adult children want only the best for their parents, my radar went up because I've seen adult children take advantage of their parents many times over the years. The dollar amount Rachel was considering was a sizable sum indeed, especially as a percentage of her net worth.

I remembered an experience I'd had seven years earlier.

BUYER BEWARE:

"Of course I'd love to meet your son, Ms. Swenson, it's usually a good idea to communicate with family about finances." Later, I came to realize that young Mr. Swenson was an exception to this rule. We scheduled an appointment for the three of us to meet in my office.

My first insight into his character came when he walked straight into my office without knocking. My receptionist was right behind him, mouthing to me that he had just walked past her, she had tried to stop him, and she was sorry.

"No problem. We'll be fine, thanks." It bothers me when clients and prospects are rude to my staff, because I like my staff and want them to be happy coming to work.

"What's your background?" were the first words out of his mouth. Clearly, this was going to be antago-nistic. But what he asked next left me speechless.

"How much will my mom's account be worth in thirteen years?"

Had I heard him right? Had he actually just asked me that? He'd researched her life expectancy and wanted to know how much he was likely to inherit when she died. My stomach turned.

While this interview had happened several years earlier, it was still fresh. So with that memory bang-ing around in my head, I asked Rachel what type of help she was thinking of giving her son, how much she planned on giving him, were there plans for repayment, and so forth.

As it turns out, her son and his wife wanted to purchase a home. They felt that the real estate market was depressed, rates were low, and they wanted to take advantage of the opportunity. All of which made sense.

In this case, I had met the son and knew for a fact that, like most children, he had his mom's best interests at heart. He was clearly not calculating his inheritance and would rather his mom be comfortable than put his own needs first.

"What do you think? Can I afford to help my son buy this house?" Rather than answer, I shared the analogy of the oxygen mask with Rachel. Recently, she had flown to New York City to visit friends and take in a show. I asked her about her flight, and asked whether they had demonstrated the safety features on the plane. Of course they did, she told me.

"What do they tell you to do when the oxygen masks fall from the ceiling?" I asked. Instantly she replied, "You put them over your face."

"Who puts theirs on first, the parents, or the children?" There was a moment of silence, during which I knew the conversation could go either way. Either she would be willing to see the point and agree with me. Or decide that she just didn't want to hear any more from the crazy financial planner who just didn't understand her situation.

After careful contemplation, Rachel said, "I'm not sure I get what you're saying." I let out a sigh of relief because I really liked Rachel and didn't want to see her poor. It sounded like she was open to suggestion regarding this large gift.

"Here's the challenge, Rachel. Wanting to help your children is a normal, natural desire. I'm willing to give up everything to help my daughters. But the problem, you see, is that we've discovered that you're not in a position financially to help them to that degree."

I continued, "What would likely happen is that you would be helping them now but in a few short years you would run out of money and be forced to make some hard decisions. You might even be forced to move in with them. My guess is that this is not where you want to end up. Am I right?"

"So you don't think I can afford to give them money?" One of the things I liked about Rachel was her forthrightness and honesty.

"Rachel, whether you give your children money is really not my business. I understand the impulse and would support you whatever you do. We can do financial planning in a vacuum where our emotions don't come into play, but in real life we need to consider more than just the hard facts.

"But to answer your question, I don't believe you can give your children that much money based on what I know about your financial situation. Might it be possible to help them, but to a lesser extent?"

With that we had a lengthy dialogue regarding the wisdom of helping her son in such a significant way financially.

I often run into clients like Rachel who are willing to listen and modify their plans based on a professional opinion. Unfortunately, not everyone is like her.

Frequently I see parents helping their children purchase homes, cars, education, even Karate lessons sometimes to their own financial detriment. Can you afford to help your children financially?

Before doing anything, ask yourself if they really need your help? Or do they want your help? Big difference.

Then go through the financial planning process. If you help your children now, might that place you in the perhaps unwanted and awkward position of needing to move in with them later? Is that acceptable?

Might you be placing the oxygen mask on their faces first? Before your own? There is nothing wrong with placing your own legitimate needs first. After all, the odds are that your children have time to make more money. Do you?

If, on the other hand, they need money because they handle money poorly, will giving them more really help?

When might you give your children money without a second thought? If you have such a large net worth that you could afford to give that money away and never see it again and it wouldn't affect your lifestyle in the slightest, this might make sense. Or perhaps your financial advisor and attorney have recommended giving your children money as an estate planning technique. There are always special circumstances, of course.

Is there a simple formula that will guide you in making this decision? None that I know. As you've guessed, I'm an advocate of hiring professional help. A good financial planner can help you decide what, if any, help you can afford to give your children.

What about loaning your children money? Loaning money to your children is OK as long as you don't need the money back. Ever.

What about co-signing for a loan for your children? Think carefully before assuming this responsibility. If for any reason they are unable to repay the loan, your good credit will be damaged.

Claire was surprised when her car insurance went up for no apparent reason. Upon inquiring, she learned that her daughter had been one day late on a car loan. Unfortunately, Claire had co-signed on the loan for her daughter so both of them experienced a decline in their credit ratings. Claire didn't know that her automobile insurance company took her credit record into account when determining her insurance rate, thus the increase in her automobile insurance rate.

If your son or daughter is late on payments, creditors may even come after you and your assets. Tread cautiously when taking this very big step.

SUMMARY

Before obeying the natural instinct to help your children financially, ask yourself, "Can I afford to lose this money? Might this gift ultimately lead to my being forced to move in with my children? Who has the ability to earn more money in their lifetime, them? Or me?"

Chapter 2

HOW TO INVEST LIKE A BILLIONAIRE

Driver: "I don't know how I hit the pedestrian, he just appeared out of nowhere."

Judge: "But he was crossing at a crosswalk. How could you miss him?"

Driver: "Well, I was steering by looking in my rear-view mirror, like always. He stepped out in front of me. "

A judge is unlikely to have much compassion for this driver, don't you think? After all, who drives by looking in the rear-view mirror? It's crazy to think that watching the road behind will allow you to anticipate what's ahead, isn't it?

And yet many, maybe most, individual investors do exactly that. How?

Investors often "drive," or make their investment choices, based on what happened in the past. They see an investment that performed well over the past six months, year, or longer and figure they want to get on that train. Or they read in a magazine about an investment that did well recently, maybe even receiving a high rating from a reviewer, and they figure it's a winner.

This is what is known as extrapolating. Extrapolation is defined as "To infer or estimate by extending or projecting known information." An example would be to follow this sequence of numbers 2, 4, 6, 8, 10, 12… If we were asked what the following number would be, the answer is easy to infer, the next number in the sequence would be 14.

But here's where it gets ugly. When it comes to investing, there is no regular pattern, no way to infer where the markets will go next. Purchasing investments based on where they were in the recent past won't help us much.

So we pick up a magazine at the newsstand, we read that a given investment has done well recently, and we decide we want to get onboard. We invest and soon the value goes down and we ask ourselves, "What happened? Am I just unlucky?"

What happened is that different sectors and niches in the markets, called "asset classes," do well at different times and for different reasons. They leapfrog over one another, but not in any order. In this case, we may have bought into a recent trend, just before it was ready to flatten out and perhaps even trend down. Wouldn't it be nice if we could tell in advance which sectors of the market were going to be the leaders in the coming months or years? Alas, it doesn't work that way.

In addition to the pain that goes with losing money, another reason this experience can be so damaging is that investors will sometimes decide that they're just unlucky, and refrain from investing again. They receive all the downside, with none of the upside. It's like dieting by cutting out ice cream and sweets, then gaining weight. It just all seems bad.

Don't lose heart. The odds are good that you're not unlucky, cursed, or necessarily a poor investor. You just need some education and perhaps an experienced advisor to lean on.

If buying five-star investments isn't necessarily the best way to go, what then?

We often hear that big institutions, such as endowments and public pensions, enjoy higher returns on their investments than individual investors. These are organizations that have millions, even billions to throw around, and we might tell ourselves that it's their size that makes them successful. But really, it's their investment approach, their discipline, their methodology, that makes them successful.

So let's look at how institutions invest and see what regular individual investors can learn from them.

ASSET ALLOCATION

Suppose you hired an experienced landscape contractor to design your yard. Your instructions to her went something like this: "I would like to be able to look outside year round and see flowers blooming. I always want color in my yard. Please find plants that bloom at different times of year."

In investment parlance, what you've described are plants that are "non-correlated," meaning that they don't all bloom at the same time. Investments that are non-correlated increase in value on their own schedule, not in lockstep with other asset classes.

Now consider that institutions, such as endowments, public and private pensions and other large organizations earn significantly more on their investments than individual investors. In fact, according to Dalbar, a company that studies such things, institutions earn somewhere between 10 percent and 12 percent on their investments over multiple years.

Dalbar also found that individual equity investors earn less than 4 percent annually.

That is a VERY big difference.

What explains this discrepancy? There are several

factors, including risk tolerance, discipline, time horizon and fees. But more important than all these combined is the asset allocation approach that institutions employ when investing.

Asset allocation is the practice of determining what percentage of our money will be placed in which asset classes. It's like that garden where you decide which plants you want to include, and how much of the garden you'll devote to those plants.

Say we sprinkle our investment choices a bit, a little in this asset class, a little in that asset class. The amount we place in each asset class is important and it can't be done without serious forethought and planning. But the basic idea is to arrive at an asset allocation model that fits our risk tolerance, time horizon, income needs, family situation, goals and so forth.

How do institutions address this issue of asset allocation? How are they able to remove the emotion that drives most individual investor's decisions?

Institutions rely on a document called an Investment Policy Statement. The Investment Policy Statement (IPS) dictates how the institution's investments will be divided up. Once it's written, the board of trustees is responsible for ensuring that the IPS is followed to the letter. Otherwise, the trustees might become liable for losses in the portfolio.

In essence, here is the way it works: the IPS directs that the money in the investment portfolio be divided up into pieces, called asset classes. Each asset class must make up a certain percentage of the portfolio. The board of trustees is responsible for ensuring that the portfolio follows the Investment Policy Statement. On a regular basis, at least annually, the board is responsible for rebalancing the portfolio.

This is perhaps the single most important reason that institutions enjoy higher returns in their investments than individuals. What makes this so important?

To answer that, let's see how many investors behave. If an investor owns two investments for one year, one will outperform the other, without exception. What does the investor then do? In some cases, they sell the investment that is doing poorly and buy the investment that is doing well.

The institution, on the other hand, sells off enough of the better performing investment to bring it back in line within the range allowed by the IPS.

Then, and here is where it gets sticky, the institution will buy more of the poorly performing investment to bring it back into the range dictated by the IPS.

To get a sense of just how counter-intuitive this is, imagine this scenario: You've been approached by a financial advisor. He tells you he has two investments to offer, one has enjoyed a sizable increase over the last year, the other a sizable loss. He thinks you should buy the loser. You think he's the loser.

In actual practice, we as individuals simply cannot step up to the plate and buy investments that have poor recent performance. We want to "watch it for a while and see how it does." We understand the concept of "buy low, sell high," but emotionally we just can't seem to do it.

Institutional managers, on the other hand, have no choice. They have to follow the discipline as outlined in the IPS, without emotion, without regret, without second guessing.

BUYER BEWARE:

Sam set his coffee cup on the table and leaned back in his chair as he shared his story. He carefully considered his words, "Both my rich neighbor and my tax guy told me that I should just buy an investment tied to a popular index. The investment offered low fees and broad diversification, not to mention great performance over the last five years. It seemed like a no-brainer to me."

At this point, Sam went quiet. His investment hadn't worked out quite the way he had hoped and he was worried. He was also a little embarrassed, feeling responsible for his decision.

Sam was hurting financially despite having retired with a little over $1 million just two years earlier.

At the beginning of 2008, at age 65, Sam hit his goal of a million dollars in savings and retirement accounts. From these funds, he had read that he could draw approximately 4 percent, or $40,000 per year ($3,333 per month) in income. Added to his Social Security of approximately $24,000 per year ($2,000 per month) Sam enjoyed a pretax income of $5,333 per month. Sam set his budget accordingly.

By the end of 2008, his $1 million had declined in value to approximately $630,000. Based on the same withdrawal rate of 4 percent, Sam could now only expect to receive $2,100 per month from his investments. Added to his Social Security income of $2,000 per month, Sam would now receive $4,100, less than he required to pay his bills.

In twelve short months, Sam went from feeling that he was living on easy street to wondering how long his money would last, now that he is eating into principal a little bit each month. This will only get worse because eating into principal creates a downward spiral. A lower and lower balance creates a lower and lower "safe" withdrawal rate.

Sam is in trouble, and there's no silver bullet, no magic solution. If he had employed a disciplined asset allocation strategy implementing the institutional process, he might have been in much better shape.

SUMMARY

Institutions, such as endowments and pensions, earn more on average than individual investors. They do this not because they're larger, but because they use a disciplined investment strategy dictated by their Investment Policy Statement. Individual investors could potentially benefit from imitating the institutions and develop their own Investment Policy Statement which they may modify over time, but from which they never stray. This will help them avoid the emotions that can torpedo their best intentions. By employing a disciplined approach individual investors could potentially succeed.

Chapter 3

DON'T DISINHERIT YOUR CHILDREN BY ACCIDENT

Kari Kennedy couldn't believe her ears. She was shocked, outraged, dumbfounded, at a loss for words. The Supreme Court of the United States had just decreed that her own father, William Kennedy, had disinherited her when he died in 2001 and left the money in his retirement account to his second wife whom he had divorced in 1994.

Kari was doubly confused because she was holding her father's divorce decree signed by the ex-wife Liv Kennedy, in which Liv signed away her interest in William's retirement account. The agreement had been filed with the court and was binding.

Even so, the Supreme Court held that Liv, the ex-wife, would receive the balance of William's 401(k) retirement plan, worth well over $400,000.

Shocking! How could such a thing happen?

Was it because William and Liv had been married for more than twenty-two years? Did that give Liv rights to his retirement plan? No. Was there perhaps a fight between William and his daughter Kari? Perhaps he meant to disinherit her? No. In fact William Kennedy had every intention of leaving his estate to Kari, including the 401(k) balance. Kennedy went to his grave thinking that Kari would receive his retirement account and its hundreds of thousands of dollars.

So what happened?

When Kennedy divorced his wife, both of them signed the divorce decree wherein they divided up their money. No doubt she received assets, perhaps the house and a car. One of the assets that he retained was his 401(k) retirement plan.

But twenty-seven years before he died, way back in 1974, William had walked into the human resources department at DuPont, his employer, and had asked for a change of beneficiary form. On this document he had designated Liv Kennedy, his bride of just three years, as his primary beneficiary. He did not indicate any contingent beneficiary, not even his daughter from his previous marriage, Kari.

I can see William now, racing into the HR department, in a hurry, distracted, thinking about all the items on his to-do list that day. He might have sat down then and completed the form, filling in Liv's name, her date of birth, and perhaps her Social Security number.

Then he came to the section of the form labeled "Contingent Beneficiary." William thought about his young daughter but probably didn't have her Social Security number with him. Or perhaps he was just in a hurry. Or maybe the Human Resources person helping him didn't know the importance of keeping beneficiary forms up to date.

Kennedy probably meant to go back and finish the form, but he may have just gotten busy and never returned to complete it.

In the end, though, this didn't really matter. Because regardless of whether the beneficiary form listed Kari as contingent beneficiary or not, Liv was still living when William died.

And there's the rub. When he divorced Liv in 1994, *he never went back and updated the beneficiary form* for his 401(k) retirement plan. So when he died in 2001, Liv was still listed as the primary beneficiary.

When his employer, DuPont, received the death certificate, they simply followed the instructions Kennedy had given back in 1974 and had never modified. They wrote a check from William's retirement account to his only heir.

Liv. The former wife.

Kari sued DuPont, claiming that Liv had waived her right to the proceeds in the divorce agreement. DuPont argued they had followed the instructions on file. DuPont won in the end.

Why? Because of a law known as ERISA, the Employment Retirement Income Security Act, which was passed by Congress in 1974 to standardize the rules regarding retirement plans such as 401(k)s. This law trumps most other laws and agreements and certainly wins out over divorce decrees.

If William had simply walked in to the human resource department at DuPont after his divorce and said, "I'd like to update my beneficiary form for my 401(k) so that my daughter is my primary beneficiary," Kari would have been sitting pretty. Instead he didn't update the form and his ex-wife inherited monies earmarked for his daughter.

William Kennedy could have made any of several possible mistakes. Here are some things I think may have happened, because I've seen each dozens of times.

For instance, once he had his divorce decree in hand, the one where Liv signed away her rights to the retirement plan, William might have simply thought that it was taken care of with nothing left for him to do.

Or it could be that he went into the human resources

department to get a new beneficiary form, saw a long line, and decided to come back later. But like all of us, he got busy and then he forgot. Perhaps he took the form home with him, with every intention of completing it and bringing it back the next day.

Or maybe he sent his document in, and the clerk behind the human resources counter threw it away by accident. William didn't think to follow up. The rest is history.

He might have thought that his attorney would handle it, but unfortunately, that isn't the attorney's job. Only the plan participant, in this case William, can change the beneficiary on his account. Maybe William had a living trust or a will and assumed that this controlled the retirement plan but he was mistaken.

This happens much more often than we'd like to think. Beneficiary forms are not updated for all sorts of documents and reasons. We get busy, we forget, we mean well, and we don't do it, with serious consequences.

What's sad is that mistakes like this are often made when investors are trying to save a penny, like the old saying, "penny-wise but pound-foolish." Perhaps a few dollars were saved by not hiring an estate planning attorney. Maybe they didn't see the value in working with a financial advisor. It might even be that whichever company holds their investments has a policy that changes their beneficiary designations arbitrarily (as one large investment company did a few years ago).

Regardless, the end result is that hundreds, thousands, sometimes millions of dollars which should have ended up in the hands of the children or other rightful heirs, instead lands in some unintended places.

PRO RATA VERSUS PER STIRPES (PRONOUNCED 'PER STIR PEAS'):

Ada's IRA was her largest asset. Her plan was to leave it in equal proportions to each of her three children, Sarah, Tom, and Hannah, at her death. She also wanted to care for her children's spouses and their children. She didn't know that the beneficiary document she signed when she opened the account indicated 'pro rata' by default. Unfortunately, the financial advisor who provided the form didn't know either.

Sadly, Ada's middle child Tom died at a time when Ada herself was in poor health. Tom and his wife, Elizabeth, had three children whom Ada adored. Ada had intended to help Tom and Elizabeth's children through college.

Shortly thereafter, Ada herself died, without updating her beneficiary form.

What happened to Ada's IRA account balance? It was divided equally between her surviving children,

Sarah and Hannah.

How much went to Elizabeth and her children? Nothing. What about Ada's plan to help Tom and Elizabeth's children through college? It died with her. Elizabeth and her children received nothing from Ada's IRA account. In fact they were left in difficult financial straits by Tom's unexpected demise.

The document she signed dictated that upon her death, Ada's IRA balance would be distributed 'pro rata.' This meant that the balance was divided between the remaining living heirs of her IRA, Sarah and Hannah. Elizabeth and her children were disinherited when Ada died. That is what pro rata means.

Incidentally, part of the reason Ada wasn't overly concerned about this issue is that her trust clearly read that her children would divide her estate and that her grandchildren would be taken care of. Unfortunately, a living trust document cannot override IRA beneficiary paperwork.

Now let's talk about Florence. Florence found herself in a similar situation with two children, Alexandra and Isabel, as well as some grandchildren. The difference is that when Florence signed her IRA documentation, she indicated that in the event of her death, she wanted the IRA account to be divided between her two children in equal shares *per stirpes*.

Interestingly, the brokerage firm where she opened her IRA account used account documentation that defaulted to 'pro rata,' but Florence found a financial advisor who was on the ball. This advisor had her alter the document to read 'per stirpes' because the advisor knew her wish was to care for her children as well as their spouses and children.

Just like Ada, Florence experienced the death of one of her children, Isabel. Isabel was divorced, but left three children, all over the age of 18. Florence never had the opportunity to update the beneficiary form on her IRA as she unfortunately died soon after Isabel.

In her case, Florence's IRA proceeds were divided as follows: her living heir, Alexandra, received half of her estate—the other half of her estate was divided equally between her three grandchildren just the way she had intended.

This is what happens when the account paperwork reads 'per stirpes.' One method is not better than the other. What's important is your individual situation. What suits you best?

This issue of pro-rata versus per stirpes is just one of many variables that we must consider when planning our estates, but it illustrates how simple it is to cut our rightful heirs out of their share of our assets when we pass.

What forms must we track regularly?

The list is long, and this is not complete, but: IRAs, Roth IRAs, SIMPLE plans, 401(k), 403(b), pension plans, annuities of all kinds, life insurance, trusts, wills, transfer on death accounts, joint tenant accounts… there's more, but you get the picture. Someone has to track all of these accounts that list beneficiaries and ensure that they are updated.

How often? Anytime something significant happens we should consider updating all of our beneficiary documents. Births, deaths, divorces, and when business relationships end are all good times to update beneficiary forms.

But everything should be reviewed no less than annually. Too many changes occur to let it go any longer. The best way to do this is to create a simple system to handle it. For example, keep a list of ALL the various assets you own and who is the named beneficiary. Then pick a day that you will commit to reviewing all of those documents for current accuracy. Perhaps May 1st, immediately after tax season.

At my financial planning firm, we handle this important issue by designating June as beneficiary planning month. We review all of the documents affecting our clients and discuss with them the changes that may have occurred over the last year.

BUYER BEWARE:

Stan had heard that estate taxes can be as high as fifty percent of the estate. But Stan didn't like the idea of spending money on an attorney to draw up an estate plan, so he decided to take matters into his own hands. He took the bulk of his money and purchased collectibles, mostly model planes and cars. He did this shortly before his death in an effort to avoid estate tax.

When he died, his family had absolutely no idea what anything was worth or even how to go about selling it, so they had to search for an appraiser they could trust, then go through the time consuming process of selling all that Stan had left.

Once the family finally finished the process of selling all the items, they learned that his estate was well under the limit for estate taxation. Everything he did ended up being a complete waste of time and money, not to mention aggravation for the family he left behind.

Unfortunately, investors often take self-defeating actions when they recognize their time is limited. Granted, Stan's case was extreme, but others do things that are unwise. Don't be a Stan. Hire an expert.

Estate planning is a complicated, ever-changing

arena, and the person you ultimately hire to create your estate plan documents should be a specialist. Most attorneys will tell you that they create living trusts, but if they also practice other types of law, then they may not be the best choice for estate planning. Keeping up with the latest in estate planning law is time-consuming and requires a person to be immersed in it full-time. That's why I only recommend attorneys who solely practice estate planning when estate planning is needed.

What about those prefabricated, fill-in-the-blank type documents that can be purchased online or at legal document service offices? My experience is that they cause more trouble than they're worth. They're a classic case of the 'penny-wise and pound-foolish' approach. I've seen individuals save $2,000 on their estate plan and lose hundreds of thousands of dollars because of unintended consequences caused by a poorly drafted trust.

What are some of the problems these low-price trusts might cause? Spouses and children disinherited, estates taxed unnecessarily, money spent on attorneys to straighten out the mess, on and on the list goes.

Save money by using coupons at the store, looking for the cheapest gas station, or turning your heater down a few degrees, but DON'T skimp on estate planning.

While we're at it, individuals or couples sometimes name friends and family as successor trustees in their trust documents, so let's talk next about that…

SUMMARY

Beneficiary documents are VERY important and should be reviewed at least annually. Don't choose estate planning as a way to skimp or save a few pennies. Hire an attorney who works exclusively in estate planning. Don't panic and do something impulsive, you will only hurt your heirs, not help them.

Chapter 4

AVOID UNNECESSARY TURMOIL IN YOUR FAMILY

The similarities were there. The wide set eyes, the perky nose, the squarish jaw. They were sisters, that was certain. Tammy and Susan were in their late fifties and were clearly intelligent, hard-working, kind people. Yet despite this, I sensed their unease with each other and wondered if they had always been at odds or if something had happened recently to create friction. They were in my office because their mother, who had been widowed over ten years earlier, recently died. They had financial questions and needed advice.

While they were certainly sad over their mother's death, this wasn't what caused the tension between them. It felt like an electric current was building, threatening to spark and cause a fire. They bristled at one another with barely disguised contempt.

At one point in the conversation, I asked if they had always found it difficult to get along. Each of them looked away, an embarrassed silence weighing heavily. Finally, Tammy said they had gotten along fine for most of their adult lives but the stress of managing their mom's estate had taken a toll on their relationship. Susan nodded just enough for me to know that she agreed.

It wasn't the first time I'd seen things go awry in a happy family. Nearly every time one or more children is named successor trustee(s) of their parent's estate, I witness this sort of friction.

In this case, it was even worse than one child being named successor trustee. Both Tammy and Susan had been named as successor co-trustees. And why not? Both were obviously capable, bright, responsible, mature individuals. Unfortunately, they couldn't agree on anything.

Their mother had left a small estate but had included some specific provisions. These provisions seemed easy enough to follow but it's never that simple. Tammy and Susan couldn't agree on the first thing about how to follow their mother's wishes. Add to this the strain of the time taken to administer the estate and the concern with following all legal and tax law and it was no wonder the two were at odds. As I watched them interact, I realized that Tammy was the stronger of the two, Susan being more passive. In the end Tammy got her way and made simple mistakes with their inheritance. Susan became resentful. In the end, no one was well served or happy. The sisters' relationship has been strained ever since, and that tension has carried over into the rest of their families.

If you're considering the best way to manage your wills and trusts, your first thought will probably be to select the most responsible child or children to serve as successor trustee(s). That is the most common option chosen by parents. But leaving your child or children as trustee(s), without professional assistance, can be disastrous. They and their families will almost certainly pay a heavy price.

After their parents' deaths, many, maybe most siblings, stop speaking to one another, at least for a time. Even those who once were good friends often find themselves in the unfortunate position of being disliked, distrusted, even vilified by their formerly close siblings. This is especially vexing at such a difficult time of life, when they really need to support one another emotionally.

Perhaps it won't surprise you to learn that money issues can come between even the happiest of brothers and sisters. When siblings experience conflict over money issues after the death of a parent, it doesn't mean that one sibling or another is doing anything unfair or unkind. It doesn't imply dishonesty or cheating. In fact, all involved may be perfectly honest in intent and action, but still be ostracized. The parents may very well select the most responsible of their adult children to serve as trustee while the estate is being distributed and that child may do everything in a fair and equitable fashion. And still, they will likely bear the wrath of the other heirs at some point in the process.

Here's why. The parents die, leaving "Jane" as the successor trustee of the family trust. Jane is responsible and familiar with finance, but quickly realizes that she can't find her way through the thicket of legal and tax law, so she hires an attorney and a tax professional to help. This is wise because there are many forms that need to be filed and many items that must be tracked down and accounted for and researched. The attorney and tax preparer tell Jane that there are certain timelines and guidelines they need to follow.

The odds are good, I'll even say nearly 100 percent, that at some point, Jane will be accused by the other heirs of doing something terrible. She'll be blamed for showing favoritism, even if she follows the trust document to the letter. She'll be blamed for dragging her feet and postponing the distribution of money needlessly, even if she is following the instructions of the attorney or tax professional. She'll be accused of allowing assets to depreciate while she "does nothing," even though she is working tirelessly to finalize the estate.

And all the while, Jane is exposing herself to liability in the event that she or her advisors miss something important. Consider the time she'll spend working on the estate, time she could be spending with her family or at work. Jane may use her vacation time for at least one year to care for her duties as executor or trustee. We can see why Jane might be an unhappy camper.

Naming adult children as successor trustees can be such a bad idea, I'd like to shout from the rooftops, "BEWARE! Asking your adult children to serve as successor trustees when you die is harmful to their friendships, work, family and checkbook!"

Thankfully, there's a simple fix. It's possible to create an atmosphere where the siblings are all in agreement, not fighting among themselves, regardless of the size of their parent's estate. Parents who own a large estate can name a corporate co-trustee to assist their children in managing the estate after their death. The American Bar Association says any estate over $500,000 or so would benefit from the services of a professional trustee. You want a successor trustee who is financially sound, stable, responsible and without any conflicts of interest. It's likely that your current financial advisor is associated with a trust company. One advantage to using your current financial advisor's trust department is he or she already knows your situation. They might even know your children and can simplify the process for everyone. Or you might look to a bank that offers trust services.

When naming a corporation such as a bank or trust company as a co-trustee, parents accomplish several objectives at the same time. First, they remove liability from the shoulders of one or more of their children. Second, they ensure that all applicable tax and other requirements will be followed by someone experienced and licensed in these matters. Finally, and maybe most important, they create an environment where their heirs are united in a unique way. The heirs/children may not agree with the corporate trustee but at least they'll all be on the same side of the table. The corporate trustee can serve as the common enemy if there are disagreements.

The best scenario, from a legal perspective, is to name a corporate trustee as the only successor trustee, but most folks like to include their children in some fashion.

While each situation is unique, the benefits of naming a corporate trustee can apply in almost any circumstance. Corporate trustees have professional knowledge and expertise in the administrative complexities of trust management and employ professionals who have the time, expertise and resources to help achieve better results than an individual family member trustee. They provide accurate reporting with periodic statements and customized reports, are regulated and monitored by government agencies and are held to a much higher standard than individual trustees. Corporate trustees have a perpetual lifespan, while individual trustees must name successors in the event of death, incapacitation or incompetence. Most important, corporate trustees are objective and can reduce strain on a family.

Search for one that offers the flexibility you desire. For example, some may be willing to handle certain administrative duties, while allowing a family member to make most of the hard decisions. Others may be willing to take over much of the administrative work and also make the difficult decisions that come whenever a large estate is divided.

One client told me about her distaste for using a corporate trustee as successor trustee. She told me a story about a family she knew where the parents had left a corporate trustee in charge and all the kids had been united in their dislike for this "meddlesome" party.

I told her it was better to have the heirs united in their dislike for a corporate trustee than be united in their dislike for one of their own. She agreed.

If you feel you'd rather your heirs not have to pay the

fees to a trust company to help manage your accounts, consider this: If they don't have a trust department to lean on, your heirs are going to need to hire an attorney. I don't see that as an advantage. To enlist the help of a trust department, interview several, then have your estate planning attorney include language in the trust that names the trust department you select as co-trustee. The trust company will provide the specific language the attorney must use. My experience is that trust company fees are minor in comparison to the value they add.

Finally, perhaps the most important thing you can do is communicate with your heirs, particularly your partner. Including children in the loop is generally a good idea.

Some families have one person who simply cannot be included in the discussions about finances. We just have to live with that. But if there are other children, perhaps the one(s) who will serve as (co) successor trustees, fill them in on your financial picture. Perhaps you don't feel comfortable sharing every detail but at least give them an overview of what they'll be facing once they inherit your assets.

The language in the trust can be such that if the siblings are united in disliking the corporate trustee, they have the ability to fire them and hire another. In this way, they're not stuck with a trust company or trust officer they don't like. Everyone wins.

SUMMARY

Be kind to your children and friends. Don't expect them to quit their job to care for your estate (if over $500,000). Hire a professional trust company to do that job. Name a corporate trust department as trustee or co-trustee.

Chapter 5

HOW WOULD I SELECT AN ADVISOR FOR MY MOM?

If I were no longer able to care for my mother's finances, how would I go about finding her an advisor in her hometown of Ann Arbor, Michigan, 2,300 miles from my home in California? What criteria would I use, what process of elimination?

If you're in the market for a financial advisor, you'll be able to follow these steps and confidently find an advisor.

For me, this would be a two-step process. First I would cast a wide net, looking at all the possible candidates and then narrow it down until I had a manageable group of potentials. Second, I would decide how to actually interview potential advisors so that I could find the one that fits the situation best.

It's a bit like dating. I've often thought dating would

be much easier if everybody just donated a blood sample to a central agency and then individuals were all matched up by chemistry. Chemistry is an elusive thing, hard to pin down, sometimes one person is feeling it, the other is not. The same holds true for finding an advisor. Do you have "chemistry?" Do you like this person? More important, can he or she do a good job with your finances?

My average client has been with me well over a decade, longer than many marriages last, so I think it's fair to compare this process to courtship. Couples usually take time to get to know one another before tying the knot. After all, they hope to be together for a while, don't they? You hope to work with your advisor for life, I would assume, so why not give this process the time it deserves? Not months or years, but certainly you would want to meet that person more than once, wouldn't you? Nobody wants to get stuck with someone unqualified. Not in marriage and not in a client/planner relationship.

I've asked investors over the years what drew them to their current advisor and here are some of the most common answers:

- Good parking.
- Nice office.
- Attended a free lunch seminar.
- First floor office.

- My rich uncle uses them.
- I know the receptionist.
- They sent me a postcard offering their services.
- I'm diversified, I have accounts with different companies.
- My CPA recommended him or her.

The last answer is the only one that has any validity. CPAs can be a good resource for referrals. All of the other answers may not be the best reasons to hire an advisor.

Now that I'm beginning my search for an advisor for my mom, I would insist that she work with a Certified Financial Planner (CFP). The hurdles to becoming a CFP are considerable. First, anyone earning the designation today has to have at least a bachelor's degree, three years of full-time experience in financial planning, and must complete the educational requirement, which takes most individuals between eighteen months and three years to complete. The student then sits for an intense ten-hour exam designed to challenge his or her working knowledge of topics such as investment management, estate planning, taxation, insurance and so forth. Finally, the CFP Board runs a background check on all prospective participants. Only after successfully completing these steps may the candidate begin using the CFP designation.

Once a person earns the CFP designation, they must complete thirty hours of continuing education every twenty-four months, so you know they're staying current.

In 1999, I found myself with over a decade of experience in the stock brokerage business, working at one of the largest brokerage firms on the planet, facing an increasingly complicated world. I had to make a decision: evolve, develop, progress, or get left behind. I set myself on the task of finding the most advanced, comprehensive, useful educational program I could find, and the CFP (Certified Financial Planner) certification course was it. After several years of classes and some difficult tests, I was awarded the Certified Financial Planner designation in 1999 and have been proud to carry it ever since.

What about a referral from my mom's tax preparer? This is sometimes a great way to find a good advisor, if the tax preparer is someone established in the community with lots of ties to local professionals. But the financial advisor must still have the proper credentials.

In this case I asked my mom about getting a referral from her tax preparer. She doesn't have much of a relationship with her tax person because her situation is simple and she doesn't know him well, so if I was really looking to help her, I'd have to do my own research.

In order for this process to seem real, I acted as if I really was searching for a CFP in my mom's area. I started by going to www.cfp.net and clicking on the box that says "Find a CFP Professional." Then, I entered her zip code and selected 'within 25 miles' and received over 300 results, so I reduced it to five miles. This gave me sixty-three CFP certificants from which to choose. I eliminated any that had a disciplinary history, which can be found by typing their last name and state into the CFP Board's website (none did). I needed to weed out the crowd. Note: Investors do not need to work with someone local, but I knew my mother wanted someone nearby.

In my (decidedly informal) search in Ann Arbor, I found CFPs at banks, brokerage firms, and independent planning firms, the three main channels we can look to for financial advice. If I didn't recognize the name of the firm, I'd look at their website.

Next, before actually communicating with these potential advisors, I would visit www.finra.org and run his or her name through the "Broker Check" feature. FINRA (Financial Industry Regulatory Authority) is the self-regulatory organization that is responsible for licensing stockbrokers. It tests prospective representatives who wish to advise investors about their investments, registers those who qualify, and then tracks each representative's career.

If a financial consultant had issues listed on their record, does that mean I wouldn't use them as a financial advisor? Not necessarily. Many advisors who have been licensed for decades will at some point receive complaints from investors that may go on their records whether or not the complaint is legitimate. I'm just looking to see how many complaints they've experienced and what were the nature of the complaints. If the advisor has the same complaints listed over and over on his or her record, this might send up a red flag. Are the issues customer complaints? For example, was the advisor repeatedly accused of improper trading?

If my list of advisors was still too large, I would further narrow it by only looking at advisors who have websites I can review. This will hopefully allow me to get a sense of their investment style, the type of clients they work with and whether they might be a good fit for my mom.

Now comes the part that requires some work, the interview. I would then call each individual on my list and ask them a series of questions that will enable my mom to make a good decision. The ones with the last names beginning with 'A' usually get all the calls so I'd start with a letter in the middle of the alphabet and begin dialing.

Here are the questions I'd ask:

1) How long have you been working with investors?

In my opinion, the minimum answer here is ten years. MINIMUM! I'd prefer fifteen, but I'll take ten. One of the most common complaints about financial advisors is that they quit the profession or move on to another firm. So you're left constantly searching for a new advisor, or being assigned an advisor at random. As a follow-up, I'd ask how long they've been with their current firm, and where they were before this. I just want to feel like there's some stability. I don't want my mom having to go through this search process repeatedly.

2) What designations do you have besides Certified Financial Planner?

ChFC, which stands for Chartered Financial Consultant is a good one to look for. CLU, Chartered Life Underwriter is a well-respected designation, but it also means that they're going to be insurance-oriented, so that may or may not be a good fit. Certified Public Accountant-Personal Financial Specialist (CPA-PFS) is another respected designation. The CPA designation is well respected, but if we were going to use a CPA as a financial advisor, I would want to be certain that investments are his or her main business focus, not tax preparation. This is a sample list of designations and is not a complete list of available credentials an advisor may have.

3) What professional affiliations do you have? To which organizations do you belong? Are you on any boards, perhaps a non-profit? Where I live, it's a small, close-knit community, and most professionals serve on a board and give back to the community. Are they in Rotary or some other service organization?

This might give me some insight into their philosophy.

4) May we speak to two clients with whom you've worked for over ten years?

I don't expect to get the names and numbers today, because the advisor likely needs to call them to ask their permission, but this shouldn't be a problem.

5) Do you sell annuities? If so, what percentage of your business is annuities?

My personal preference is that annuities make up less than 50% of the advisor's practice.

6) What is your strategy for working with your client's tax professional?

I'd want to be sure this advisor coordinates my mom's affairs with her tax preparer, otherwise how would they know when to take gains or losses for tax purposes? A good advisor can often offset their fee simply by being aware of your situation and saving you money on taxes. They should have a system in place whereby they contact their clients' tax professionals before year end, and perhaps again before April 15. Tax harvesting, tax deferral, tax free investing, delaying capital gains, maximizing retirement plans and gifting are just a few of the many things a good advisor can do to help with your tax situation. It's unfortunate when an investor will work diligently to save one half of 1 percent on their investment costs by doing it themselves, then give up fifteen percent or more of their portfolio because they make uninformed choices when it comes to taxation. I want my mom's financial advisor to have a system in place whereby he or she contacts her tax professional at appropriate times during the year.

7) How do you charge for your services?

There are several ways a financial advisor might be compensated. He or she may just receive a salary from their employer. Or they may charge a commission to buy and sell stocks or bonds on your behalf. It may be they charge hourly or a flat fee based on assets under management. They may get paid by a third party when you place your money there. Or some combination of these. Do I have a favorite? Yes, but there is no single right or wrong way to pay your advisor. My preferred method is called "fee-based." This is when the bulk of the investor's assets are invested in such a way that a fee is charged as a percentage of assets, but also allows investments in products that don't fit the "fee-only" model.

8) How did your clients do during the last market rout?

I already know the answer, some clients did better, others worse. Every client has a different risk tolerance, time horizon, income, family situation, goal, etc. So each has a different portfolio, and therefore has experienced something different. Honesty is a prerequisite, and I want an honest answer.

For the independents I'd also ask:

9) Where did you work prior to being independent and for how long? How long have you been independent? What happens to my account if something happens to you?

Most advisors got their start working for big firms, they built their client list, then left to open an independent firm. I just want a feel for their history.

Independent advisors should have a succession plan in place so that their clients are cared for seamlessly if the advisor is unable to service the account.

Here we are then, we've looked at a broad selection of financial advisors, narrowing down the list by looking at their professional designations. We've called and asked a series of questions that will allow us get a feel for the individual advisor's practices. Next I'm going to ask my mom to go see at least three and spend thirty minutes or so with each of them to gauge how she feels about working with them on an ongoing basis.

Finally, we're going to decide on whom she felt the most comfortable with.

Sometimes we're willing to spend large amounts of time planning a vacation or picking out a cell phone. Doesn't it make sense to approach the issue of selecting a financial advisor with even more care?

SUMMARY

When choosing an advisor, good parking or a free meal are not the best criteria. Ask your tax professional for a referral. Look for professional designations, such as CFP or ChFC. Find someone with at least a decade's experience. Ask them tough questions. Then ask yourself if you like and trust this person.

Chapter 6

DIWORSIFICATION

In an uncommonly courteous move, the Internal Revenue Service wanted Gloria to keep her $100,000, but nobody told her about it until it was too late. She dutifully wrote a check to the Treasury Department to pay her taxes, blissfully unaware that if she had only known, she could have trimmed her tax bill significantly simply by selling some investments that were held at a capital loss to offset capital gains she had taken.

How did this happen? Gloria diworsified.

This is her story.

Gloria knew the basic principle of diversification, and she did what she thought best. She divided her assets between two national brokerage firms, half to one, half to the other.

This is not what the word 'diversify' means. Merriam Webster says that to diversify means "To balance (as an investment portfolio) defensively by dividing funds among securities of different industries or of different classes."

When you hand over your money to an advisor, he or she takes you through a process whereby you indicate how much risk you want to take, what your time horizon is, what your goals are for your investments, age, income, liquidity needs, and so forth. Then the advisor suggests investments that, he or she believes, will suit your specific situation.

But if you give each advisor the same information, and they implement a strategy based on your profile, might they not come up with similar portfolios? They may very well purchase very similar investments, maybe even exactly the same investments, thereby eliminating the exact element of diversification you were hoping for. And that is why I call it diworsification, rather than diversification.

So to diversify in investment terms means to divide funds between actual investments, *not* between investment advisors. Dividing monies between different advisors does not guarantee diversification among "different industries or different asset classes," and it might actually result in owning the exact same, or very similar, investments across the board. In other words, it might mean doubling up on investments, the exact opposite of diversifying.

On the surface, it makes sense to divide up your assets like this, allowing two different advisors to each control a portion of your investments. "Let's give some to this advisor, some to that advisor, see how they each do." Seems reasonable. Each advisor will use his or her own investment philosophy, giving the investor diversification, right?

The truth is that many times this method is disastrous.

First, let's talk about tax ramifications. Gloria's story was mostly a tax consequence story. A story about unnecessary taxes to be precise.

Why did having two brokerage firms cost her so much? It's very simple. Gloria had realized capital gains with one firm, and unrealized capital losses with the other firm.

Why is this important? Because Gloria owed taxes on the capital gains she had generated in the one account. Another way to say this is that she had 'realized' gains. In the other account, she owned investments that reflected a loss on paper, but since she did not sell them, they are considered 'unrealized' for tax purposes.

By simply selling the investments that were at a loss, she would have "realized" the losses, and then been able to offset the "realized" gains, partially or completely erasing the tax due.

But each advisor didn't know about the other because Gloria kept them carefully separate. She felt that this was the safest way to handle her finances.

If any one person had been handling the whole lot, then that advisor could have called her and said, "Gloria, You've sold some investments at a significant profit. Let's offset the capital gains tax you've incurred by selling some of your other investments, the ones that are under water, taking the losses, and in that way minimize paying capital gains taxes." It could have been handled easily with a phone call and a minimum of expense.

If Gloria was really attached to the investments that were showing a loss, she could always have bought them back. An IRS rule disallows a loss if the security is sold, then purchased again within thirty-one days. It's called the 'wash-sale' rule. But if she had sold the investments that were held at a loss and then waited thirty-one days, she could have bought them back. Another way to implement this strategy is to sell the investments showing a loss, and buy similar (but not identical) investments in their place. In this way she could remain invested if she really wanted to.

Gloria never knew that her decision to spread her money around cost a large sum. She just dutifully paid the taxes her tax professional told her to pay. Not happily, but dutifully. Unfortunately, her tax professional responded to what happened after the fact, rather than strategizing with her prior to year end. So when she finally met with him after January 1st, the damage was done, and there was nothing she could do. In fact, he didn't even mention to her that this could have been avoided because he didn't have all the facts and didn't ask.

What a shame. Gloria has a fair bit of money but like most in her age bracket (over 60) she has what she has and doesn't expect to get any more.

Now she is $100,000 poorer and will likely never see that money again.

This issue of offsetting capital gains is just one of the many issues that costs investors money when they keep their funds with different advisors and nobody sees the big picture.

THERE IS ANOTHER, PERHAPS EVEN MORE IMPORTANT ASPECT TO THIS ISSUE OF DIWORSIFYING.

Investing successfully involves a principle called "non-correlation," which refers to the practice of purchasing investments that don't move in lock-step with one another. Non-correlated investments each move on their own schedule, which allows you the comfort of knowing that not everything in your portfolio is likely to go down at the same time should the markets decline. We might say that one part of your portfolio zigs while another zags.

A simple example of non-correlation would be to buy an interest in an umbrella company and an interest in a company that makes sunscreen. You could reasonably expect that one is doing well while the other stagnates.

If you were to look at a chart of various asset classes (e.g. "Large company stock," "International," "REIT," etc.) and how they perform over the years, you would see that one asset class rarely leads the pack for two years in a row, let alone year after year. For example, Large Company Growth Stocks might outperform one year, Corporate Bonds might be the leader the next, Real Estate Investment Trusts might be in front the year after. There is no method, schedule, rule, rhyme, or reason to how various asset classes perform or don't perform. There is no way to know in advance which asset class will take the lead. This is why successful investors give thought to how much they want to include in each of several asset classes (see Chapter 2, "How to Invest Like a Billionaire").

If two or more advisors are involved, who will see the big picture? Who can advise you on your estate plan? Who works with your tax advisor to lower your tax bill? Who helps you plan education expenses for kids or grandkids? Who do you go to for Long Term Care Insurance or other financial products you may need?

Even worse, what if there are three or more advisors involved?

One encouraging sign I've observed is that more and more investors who maintained multiple advisors while accumulating money are consolidating later in life when they're taking distributions in retirement. This becomes ever more important as we age and our risk tolerance declines, and as we accumulate ever larger estates that require careful planning to pass on to our heirs.

SUMMARY

Ask yourself if you really need two or more advisors. If you feel like you need to keep your assets with more than one advisor, then pick your favorite and make that person aware of everything. In this way you'll be less likely to experience one of the many negative issues that come with diworsifying.

Chapter 7

"BUT I OWE THEM EVERYTHING"

My popularity had just plummeted to somewhere south of zero. I could have said something trite like, 'Don't shoot the messenger,' but it wouldn't have helped. In the end, people do what they want to do and sometimes there is just nothing anyone can do to convince them differently.

Jean had been with her company for over thirty years, working her way up the corporate ladder, retiring in the summer of 1998. When she left the company, their stock was in the low $20 range and paying a generous dividend.

Jean retired owning nearly 35,000 shares of company stock, worth approximately $735,000. Jean felt like she was set, her goal of living a care-free life was about to begin, her future was bright. Now she could do all the things she had dreamed about: travel, gardening, spending time with the grandkids, volunteering, and just puttering about.

She was practically beaming with excitement when she came to see me, and why not? The company is a great American success story. In fact, my own grandfather worked there for decades before retiring. Growing up, we always owned their vehicles out of loyalty to the company—and because my grandfather received significant discounts on vehicles.

Yes, she was brimming with excitement until I gave her my opinion on her financial status. While I was genuinely happy and excited for her, too often I'd seen others in her circumstance, having worked their entire career for a large, blue chip company, accumulating their employer's stock and retiring with a large percentage of their net worth in that company's equity. Then the stock had taken a tumble, whether through mismanagement, hiccups in the economy, or industry-specific troubles, and the retiree was left in a very precarious financial situation.

"Jean, you've done a very good job accumulating funds for retirement. You worked for a great American company and should be proud of what you've achieved. I appreciate the privilege of working with investors like you who've accumulated so much by careful saving, budgeting, and investing.

"I do, however, have some concerns about the high percentage of your net worth that is tied up in one stock. While the organization is certainly a blue chip company and has been around for decades, I'm concerned that anything that may happen to them may impact your ability to live a comfortable retirement. You know, it's the old "don't keep all your eggs in one basket" principle.

"Have you given that some thought?" Then I was quiet.

Jean wasn't quiet, the words came tumbling out of her mouth as if she couldn't say it all fast enough. She told me all the reasons that it was OK for her to keep her stock. I'd heard the same arguments dozens of times from other retirees who owned employer stock.

Jean covered all the usual bases: "It's been around for many decades. I don't think it's going away anytime soon. It's the largest in the world (or second largest or whatever). They're opening up in China/India/Russia. They pay a good dividend. It's on the Dow Jones Industrial Average. They've been very good to me. I raised my family on what that company did for me. The government would never let them fail. If I sell the stock, I'll have to pay huge taxes..." On and on the reasons go.

The reality? Retirees hold on to their former employer's stock because they have an emotional attachment to it. If these same retirees were asked if someone else should keep most of their net worth tied up in one company, they would say "NO, of course not." They know intellectually it's the wrong thing to do but reason and logic fly out the window when it's their employer's stock. This is common. Human nature is a tough obstacle to overcome and it sometimes runs the show.

What happened to the stock? In 2009, more than ten years after Jean retired, the stock was trading around $2 with no dividend in sight.

How did this happen? Several reasons, but the bottom line is that even large, respected companies with decades of experience and a rich heritage can go through hard times. Your employer may be/have been the largest or oldest or most successful in its industry and yet still experience severe setbacks. In fact, I'll go out on a limb here and say that it is almost inevitable. Nearly all corporations experience a rough patch. Some come through it, some don't.

Remember Woolworth's and Montgomery Ward? How many great American corporations can you remember that no longer exist? Or exist as shells, vague memories of what they had once been?

Let me share with you one of the most important lessons of investing I've ever learned. I heard it first from my friend Don when I was in my early twenties. Don was the most successful investor I had ever met up until then and he taught me a lot. Ready?

"Don't love anything that can't love you back."

Simple, isn't it? We could apply that to any number of life's experiences but it works especially well with romance and investing. Here's the deal, your company stock doesn't know that you own it. It doesn't care that you own it. It can go to zero, leaving you penniless, and not feel even slightly guilty. It's not your friend, it won't bail you out of jail, help you move, or even give you a ride to the airport.

It's just a piece of paper. Actually, it's not even that anymore, now it's just an entry in a computer database. Why risk your financial well-being for something that can't love you, doesn't care about you, isn't even aware you exist?

Think of all the great American companies whose stock has experienced big declines, Citigroup, Xerox, American Airlines, Bank of America, Eastman Kodak, the list goes on.

What if the stock declines at the same time you need money? What if that dividend you rely on goes away? What if, what if?

An alternative? You already know the answer. Diversify.

Before selling your holdings, investigate the tax consequences, know what you're getting yourself into, but pull the trigger. Don't wait until it's too late. Often investors hold on to appreciated stock because of the tax consequences, which is a valid consideration. But saving 15 percent in taxes (the long term federal capital gains rate as I write this) doesn't make up for losing 50 percent in principal no matter how you figure it.

What happened to Jean? She chose to ignore my advice and instead took her investments (nearly all in her company stock) to a discount broker, having read that low fees meant increased returns. She held on to her stock, finally deciding to sell it when it went below $5. Because the dividend had been reduced, she had taken to selling small portions of stock to fund her lifestyle, all the while believing the stock would recover and she would come out OK.

Jean's children were unable to accommodate her in their own homes. So she now lives with her nephew in a very comfortable guest house behind his home. She is unable to travel or visit her grandchildren as much as she would like, but she does have time to volunteer and she's gotten a part-time job she seems to enjoy.

You know the old saying, "if I had a nickel for every time…" In this case, if I had a nickel for every investor who refused to diversify away from their employer's stock…. I'd have lots of nickels.

Don't commit this common, often very expensive, mistake.

BUYER BEWARE...

Pete worked for one of the largest corporations in the world, founded in America in the early part of the 20th century. Over his career he accumulated tens of thousands of shares of his employer's stock and held on to the stock when he retired. At the peak of his career he was the CFO of a multibillion-dollar corporation earning over $500,000 per year. When he retired, his pension was close to $200,000 annually. He was set, living on easy street. Or so it seemed.

He and his wife spent their days traveling, visiting the grandkids, shopping, and generally enjoying their lives.

Unfortunately, the day came some fifteen years after he retired that Pete's former employer experienced serious financial problems. After nearly one hundred years in business, the business declared bankruptcy wiping out the value of his stock, and dramatically reducing his pension.

Today, Pete is uncertain about his future. His net worth and income stream were radically reduced. What now?

In his case, Pete realized a worst case scenario where both his pension and his stock investments were tied to the same company.

Don't let this happen to you. Rather than hold on to company stock, diversify away, especially when nearing retirement. This double whammy of losing your net worth due to a decline in company stock value paired with losing part of your pension due to your former employer's economic troubles is one situation from which it is almost impossible to recover.

Now in his seventies, Pete has few options. His former lifestyle, one of freedom from financial worry, bears no resemblance to what he has today. Don't be Pete.

SUMMARY

Recognize your emotional attachment to your employer's stock for what it is. Remember the advice you've probably given others: don't keep all your eggs in one basket. Diversify.

Chapter 8

HOW MUCH CAN I AFFORD TO SPEND?

"Do you think I have enough? My rent will go up $1100 per month. Can I afford to move?"

I smiled at her. If it weren't for the genuine concern in her voice, I'd have thought she was joking. After all, with a net worth well over $5 million, certainly she could afford an additional $1,100 per month in expenses.

"Let's look at your budget and your monthly income and see how this will affect you." With that, we reviewed her investments and saw that her income was nearly $20,000 per month after taxes and that she could indeed afford rent of $5,300 per month instead of her current $4,200 per month. "Yes, Andrea, according to these numbers, you'll be just fine," I was glad to tell her.

Five million dollars seems like a lot of money, wouldn't you say? Yet even clients with a substantial net worth have asked me many times over the years if they have enough, especially if they're facing decades of retirement. Indeed, even a portfolio of millions of dollars isn't enough if invested improperly or if spending gets out of control.

If you're concerned with the possibility of running out of money, you're not alone. AARP reported on a study done by Allianz Life Insurance Company of North America. In this study of American adults ages 44 to 75, it was found that more than three in five (more than 61 percent) said they fear depleting their assets more than they fear dying.

We ask then, how much is "enough?"

The first step toward answering this question is to determine a budget. How much do you need to live on? You will probably have a similar budget to the one you have today unless something significant changes, such as the kids moving out. Many people spend more, so be realistic. You're still going to want to travel. That new car you just bought is probably not going to be "the last car you ever buy," expenses will go up, you'll want to buy things for your grandchildren and do things with your neighbors and give money to charity and remodel your home and…

Can you see why it's difficult to trim your budget drastically?

Now that we have a budget in hand that we can live with, we move to the heart of the matter. How much do

I need to sustain my lifestyle indefinitely?

Over the decades this question has been the source of heated debate. Unfortunately, no one answer fits every situation. One of the reasons it is so difficult to decide on an answer is that if the capital markets do well in the beginning of your retirement, you might be in good shape. If, however, the capital markets do poorly in the first year(s) of retirement, you might have cause for concern.

The single most common formula used to determine how much a retiree can safely withdraw from his or her portfolio and maintain their standard of living is this: add up all liquid assets and multiply by 4 percent. For this exercise a liquid asset is an investment that can be converted into cash in 30 days or less. Over the years many formulas have been presented that aim to improve on this formula. Many of these "improved" formulas may indeed be better than the 4 percent solution but they are often so difficult to implement that they're not much help.

Still, with all the various withdrawal solutions available, I want to present one more that fits my investment philosophy of imitating institutions.

It's common for endowments and other institutional investors to take a given percentage of their investment portfolios annually. But endowments typically take one step beyond the individual investor. Because they recognize that investment portfolios will fluctuate in value, they usually use some formula that takes the value of the portfolio over a pre-determined time frame.

For example, it's common for the endowment policy to say something like this, "Distributions will be 5 percent of the balance of the endowment averaged over the previous eight quarters."

This way it's not just a snapshot of one day in time, it's an average of two year's worth of balances. This tends to smooth out the bumps in income as well as take into consideration the inevitable volatility in the capital markets.

Why not imitate the institutions and implement a similar strategy? If we average the balance of our investment portfolio over the previous four quarters, then multiply that average by 4 percent, then divide by twelve we will have a dollar figure that we can reasonably expect to spend monthly for the coming three months.

Here's an example: quarter one $1,000,000, quarter two $900,000, quarter three $1,100,000, quarter four $1,050,000. The average is $1,012,500 multiplied by 4 percent = $40,500, divided by 12 = $3,375.

We could reasonably expect to be able to spend $3,375 per month for the next three months. At the end of three months, we perform this calculation again.

The purpose behind this is to smooth out the big swings in our budget somewhat while acknowledging that we do need to make adjustments periodically to keep our spending in line with movement in the capital markets.

Some factors that would change this completely? If the portfolio is entirely invested in CDs or other consistently low yielding investments, then we need to lower our expectations dramatically. CDs are highly unlikely to produce the income necessary to fund our 4 percent solution. This would be true of any fixed rate investments we might make.

So the quickest and easiest way to make a decision regarding your nest-egg and judge if it's enough? Multiply your liquid assets by 4 percent. If you can live on that number, you're probably in good shape. If not, you need to either save a little more or reduce your expenses. There aren't many other options.

SUMMARY

To estimate whether you have enough to live on, first draft a realistic budget. This is what you need annually to live on. Next, add up all liquid assets and multiply by 4 percent, then subtract taxes. This is what your investments will likely produce annually. A VERY general rule of thumb says that if these two numbers are similar, you're probably in good shape to retire.

Chapter 9

THE REAL ENEMY

Eleanor's rifle was loaded, the safety was off, and she could hear the tiger in the bushes directly in front of her. Within seconds he was coming at her, roaring fiercely. In one motion, she lifted her rifle and squeezed off a shot. She acted on instinct. Her experience paid off because with one bullet, Eleanor took him down.

Upon closer examination though, she realized she had killed a tiger cub, capable of doing damage but really just looking to play.

Meanwhile, momma tiger was coming from behind intent on protecting her baby oblivious to anything in her path. Eleanor, unfortunately, didn't hear the larger animal until it was too late and never knew what hit her.

Eleanor was prepared to stand up for herself but sadly, she didn't recognize the real enemy.

No, this is not a true story, but it does illustrate a

point. Sometimes the challenge we see in front of us, the one that seems so clear and obvious, isn't the real issue. The real issue is something else and there are times in life when we have to admit to ourselves that we don't know what we don't know.

While investors age 60 and over aren't likely to be attacked by ferocious animals, they face some very real challenges in what are sometimes called "The Golden Years." They will face various tests when it comes to investing and as time passes, the real issues may become ever cloudier. What are they?

The most obvious financial issue is safety of principal. Mark Twain purportedly was the first to say "I'm more interested in return *of* my principal, than return *on* my principal."

Who wants to return to work at the age of 80, looking to supplement Social Security? Nobody I've met. So holding on to your money is extremely important. But as with most things in life, there are trade-offs. Safety of principal to most people means bank CDs, savings accounts and money markets but using these instruments exclusively can cause serious problems for some. We'll look more closely at this. But first, let's look at the primary issue.

Will Rogers once said: "The only difference between death and taxes is that death doesn't get worse every time Congress meets." Taxes go up, taxes go down, but they don't disappear. Along with taxes, inflation is an ever-present threat that can never go away, indeed our financial system is based on the existence of a reasonable amount of inflation. The double-barreled combination of inflation and taxes, *this* is the other major financial issue facing seniors.

So, will the real enemy please stand up? Is it fluctuation of principal, or is the enemy the combination of inflation and taxes?

My guess is that you already know the answer because you've heard it on TV, from your financial advisor or you've read it in a book. Additionally, like most of us, you buy groceries and can see the value of your dollar eroding.

Inflation and taxes are the principal financial threat facing those in retirement. How did we get to the point that inflation was the principal threat to the finances of the 60 and over crowd?

Every silver lining has its cloud. In the 20th century, life expectancy went through the roof. Someone born in the year 1900 could expect to live about 48 years, but by the turn of the 21st century, that number had risen to 75. Many believe this was the most significant advancement made by humanity during the last one hundred or so years. Forget flying, electronic technology, or sending men to walk on the moon. Life expectancy made such a leap in the 20th century that all other progress pales in comparison.

This is a really good thing. But it also introduced a new and significant financial threat. All those people living all those extra years need to support themselves throughout the "golden years." In the 1950s and 1960s, the average retirement age was 67 or so and the average life expectancy was around 69. There wasn't a need for a large pool of cash to sustain individuals for decades after retirement since the retiree only needed enough cash to cover two years' worth of living expenses.

In 2009, according to the United States Census Bureau, the average retirement age was 62 and the average retiree could expect to spend eighteen years in retirement. The needs of those in retirement today are different from fifty years ago.

So an individual in his or her "golden years" is looking at the very real possibility of running out of money before he or she runs out of breath. Let's see how running out of money looks in actual practice.

With a long-term inflation rate of 3 percent (which is a reasonable expectation), a loaf of bread costing $3 today would cost the equivalent of $5.42 in twenty years.

So if you spend $500 on groceries per month now, you'll need more than $900 per month to buy the same items in twenty years. If your income is fixed, how will you make up the difference? If your investments, like CDs and other "safe" investments are not keeping up with inflation, not to mention taxes, what will you do?

Compounding the issue are the many unexpected things that happen to us along the way that eat into our principal: the kids need help buying a house, we need to replace the car we thought would last forever, extra money is required for a health issue that's not fully covered by Medicare or insurance, we decide to move to a warmer climate—the list is infinite. We find all sorts of ways to spend our nest-egg that we never expected.

Look ahead twenty years and ask yourself, "What will happen to me if I have the same amount of income and money in the bank as I do today but my expenses have doubled? How will I buy groceries? What will I have left to give my kids? How will I fund unexpected emergencies or vacations to see the grandkids? What if I want to move into a more comfortable place?"

You may have lived your entire life frugally, which I applaud, but just how much can you trim from your budget? Can you trim your expenses by half over the next twenty years?

Let's go back to our two threats. On the one hand, we have the threat of fluctuating principal. That can be solved by depositing your money into bank Certificates of Deposit (CDs) or buying U.S. Treasury bonds or T-bills. These instruments guarantee return of principal.

On the other hand, you have the threat of inflation and taxes eating away at your purchasing power over time, possibly leaving you in the awkward position of being at an advanced age with little money, stressed over paying the bills.

Surprisingly, I see some older investors shop various bank's CD rates, always looking for an extra tenth or one quarter of a percent then they make a very risky move. They find an interest rate at a bank that is just ever so slightly higher than what other banks are paying, then deposit more in that bank than the FDIC limit. Here is a person who will only buy bank CDs because they are concerned about possibly losing their principal, risking 100 percent of their deposit over the FDIC limit to earn a pittance in returns. It makes no sense.

One investor I met would only buy U.S. Treasury bonds because he didn't even trust FDIC insurance (also backed by the U.S. government, by the way). But he would also buy commodities like oil and wheat which are considered very risky investments. What kind of sense does that make? It's like claiming you want to be healthy by eating only vegetables and ice cream.

Remember Eleanor? Certainly she had every right to be concerned about the immediate threat in front of her but she missed the real enemy lurking in the bushes. Often I see individuals worry so much about exposing their assets to loss that they settle for letting their money evaporate due to inflation. What to do?

First, educate yourself. You don't need to become an expert in finance. Meet with two or three respected Certified Financial Planners and you'll learn that they each have their own take on things. There is no "right way" to invest, but you will also find that some approaches sit better than others.

Once you feel like you understand the real issues and how to address them, move ahead with confidence. Always keep some cash in reserve, six months' worth of living expenses at a minimum. If you can afford it, maybe keep a full year's worth of expenses in an FDIC-insured account with your bank or financial advisor. The rest you invest per your advisor's recommendation.

Perhaps your advisor will recommend that you stay in government-guaranteed investments. This might happen if you have so much money that you don't need to worry about your money growing over time. Or perhaps they will recommend you buy municipal bonds that in some cases pay tax-free interest. It might be that they recommend a diversified portfolio of stock- and bond-based investments. There are many approaches, each with its own advantages and disadvantages.

Next? Don't panic. If you are invested properly for the long haul, you will see your balance fluctuate from day to day, month to month. Look at it regularly but don't worry if you see it fluctuate some. If you're losing sleep over it, then perhaps tell your advisor that you want to revisit your approach when it declines a certain percentage, maybe 5 or 10 percent. That doesn't mean you'll make changes but you do want to have a conversation about it to be certain your initial approach still makes sense.

The key point to take from this chapter is that investments that seem risk-free, in the long run, may be anything but. Know your enemy, plan and plot, create a strong defense against the twin threats of inflation and taxes. Then move ahead with confidence.

SUMMARY:

While it may seem that some investments are safer because of a guarantee of principal, they may actually be riskier when inflation and taxes are factored in. Since a retiree may spend decades in retirement, it's important that his or her investments last as long as he or she does. Be prudent but be open to ideas that may allow your money to grow.

Chapter 10

TAXES—THE KEY DATE IS DECEMBER 31

Have you given up smoking? Reduced your consumption of alcohol? Perhaps you take pills to slow the buildup of plaque in your arteries in an attempt to ward off that day when neglecting your health results in some malady. It makes more sense to take care of your body now rather than to wait for a serious health issue to arise *forcing* you to make changes, right?

Taking preventive measures with your health is not unlike taking preventive measures with your finances including taxes. A little planning now can save you a lot of pain later. For example, most taxpayers set their sights on April 15th and wait until that date draws near to look at their tax situation. But by then it's too late to take advantage of many of the tax savings available. Just like our health, if we plan in advance, we can lessen the pain that comes with no planning.

YOUR TAX PREPARER, YOUR
FINANCIAL ADVISOR…AND YOU

What then are the roles of the tax preparer, the financial advisor and you? Let's start with the one person you have the most influence over, you. Your job is to take full responsibility for your finances. That doesn't necessarily mean that you must learn about taxes or investments. It does mean that you're responsible for giving careful thought to whom you hire to advise you. Hiring the right professional is critical and I've included a full chapter on just this topic. Surrounding yourself with qualified advisors may be the single most important decision you make with your finances. Have a process, select meaningful criteria, give it thought and choose well.

Rarely do the tax preparer and the client contact each other before year's end. The typical scenario is that the tax preparer is busy between January 1st and April 15th preparing taxes and handling data as they receive it from their clients. The client is busy and distracted and expects the tax preparer to ferret out all available tax savings. But by then, it may be too late for many opportunities.

After hiring professionals to assist you in making

important financial decisions, your next task is to be certain they remain interested. Everyone, including tax preparers and financial advisors, is busy. We don't want you to get lost in the shuffle. If, for example, it's the beginning of December and you haven't heard from either your tax preparer or your financial advisor, it's your responsibility to contact them and determine whether there are any actions you should take. Don't wait for them thinking they will contact you if there is any need. While it's true that, as professionals, they should contact you, things happen.

YOU must be proactive. This is why, when interviewing a financial advisor, I would ask them what system they have for contacting clients prior to year end. Their answer must give me a sense that they've given this some thought.

Your responsibility also extends to keeping neat and accurate records. It doesn't have to be fancy. A small box with hanging file folders, each labeled legibly, will suffice. You might keep one folder labeled "Accountant." Throughout the year, as you receive tax-related papers, slip these into this folder and at year's end simply hand the folder's contents to the accountant.

While I encourage you to hire professionals to assist you with your financial picture, at the same time, you don't want to abdicate responsibility.

What is the role of the financial advisor? His or her duty is to coordinate your entire financial picture. If your financial advisor is simply a "stock-picker," then he or she may not be able to assist you much in this regard. If you sense this, my suggestion would be to search for a different advisor. Hopefully your financial advisor is qualified to look at your entire financial picture and give you ideas that will ultimately save or make you money. The purpose of hiring a financial advisor is to come out ahead financially, right? You shouldn't end up worse off financially.

While we've decided that you're ultimately responsible, your financial advisor is the one who should be contacting both you and your tax preparer, ensuring that everything is accomplished before year end that needs to be accomplished.

Ideally, your tax preparer would do the same. My experience is that some tax preparers are not that proactive. It's not in their business model to pursue clients for updates. They usually wait until after the first of the year when we give them our paperwork. Typically, we'll rely on our financial advisor to get things moving.

Just be certain that somebody gets the ball rolling. You, the financial advisor, the tax preparer, somebody.

BUYER BEWARE:

Jane didn't realize that her stockbroker at the bank had taken tens of thousands of dollars in short-term capital gains during the course of 2010.

I asked her on December 1st to gather data from the stockbroker to determine if there was any tax planning we could do before year end. On December 29, she finally heard back from him when he disclosed the short term gains. What would have happened if the end of the year had passed without proper planning? Short term capital gains are taxed at the taxpayer's income tax bracket instead of the current long term capital gains tax of 15 percent. Jane's income tax bracket is 25 percent.

We quickly searched through all of her investments, with the goal of offsetting the realized capital gains with capital losses. We found that Jane had unrealized losses in her portfolio available to offset the gains. By selling these investments and realizing the losses for tax purposes, she was able to reduce her net capital gain reported to the IRS. Jane has a sizable portfolio and she accumulated these funds by being careful with her money.

Was it necessary for him to have purchased stocks, then to have sold them in less than twelve months?

Might he have held on to these stocks longer than twelve months, creating a long term capital gain rather than a more expensive short term capital gain? We don't know.

We've seen investors pay as much as $100,000 in unnecessary tax simply because they were not aware of the tax consequences.

Tax harvesting, the practice of matching gains and losses to minimize tax, is something we can accomplish before year end. In fact, it must be done before December 31st or it's too late.

What other items can we address before year end? How about IRA contributions? If you are familiar with the rules surrounding IRAs, you know that taxpayers have until April 15th of the subsequent year to make their IRA contributions for the previous year. Most taxpayers wait until the last moment to make their contributions. But this is usually a mistake. By making your IRA contribution earlier in the year, rather than waiting until the last possible moment your funds will have that much more time to grow tax-deferred. I recommend that investors make their IRA contributions in January for that year. For example, your 2012 contribution would be made in January 2012, not April 15th 2013. In this way, you benefit from the potential current tax savings as well as the additional time that your monies are invested.

If you're employed, as some seniors are, what about contributing to a retirement plan at work? In 2012, someone above the age of 50 could contribute $22,000 to a 401(k) plan at work. The problem again is that if we wait until after January 1st to start thinking about deductions for the prior year, it's too late. Even if you can only contribute 1 percent of your paycheck to a retirement plan, do it! It especially makes sense to take advantage of any match your employer provides. As time passes, you may be able to increase your contribution amount.

What if you're semi-retired but own a business? There are many opportunities to take deductions, but many are only available if you make decisions before year end. Ask your tax preparer what you can do and get on it before December 31. There may be some purchases you can make for your business that will save you money on taxes. Or perhaps you can establish a retirement plan that will allow you and your employees to make tax-deductible contributions.

If you're afraid of the expense and complexity of starting a 401(k) plan, consider instead a SIMPLE plan. The paperwork and expense are minimal and there is none of the year-end testing that makes other defined contribution plans unwieldy. There is a matching contribution portion to a SIMPLE, but it's just that, matching. This means that if employees don't contribute, the employer need not contribute on their behalf. SIMPLE plans must be established before October 1st, again emphasizing the need to plan well before December 31st.

The key here is to take advantage of as many tax-savings opportunities as possible before it's too late.

SUMMARY

A good financial advisor and tax preparer will both communicate with you before year end to determine whether there are any opportunities for savings by using such techniques as tax harvesting.

Chapter 11

"LOOK AT THIS MESS"

"Look at this mess." Wilma wasn't kidding, paperwork was everywhere. It looked like a tornado had run right through the middle of the house blowing folders, ledgers, documents and files all over the place. It was a disaster.

Her late husband, Harry, had been a good man, loved by all, a good father, husband and friend. In his lifetime he had traveled the world, met many interesting people and been financially successful. Harry had felt a responsibility to care for his wife and children, a job he did well. This inclination to take care of things was admirable...but now it was, in a way, disastrous.

After Harry died, neither his wife, daughter, nor myself, could make sense of his finances.

We found multiple checkbooks, most with no recent statements. There were several insurance policies with a confusing list of beneficiaries. In some files, reference was made to stock and bond accounts, partnerships, real estate holdings and other investments with no supporting documentation.

We couldn't tell if these various vehicles were still owned or had been sold or transferred. We made several phone calls the first day and found that much of the paperwork was obsolete but there was no way to tell what was current and what was old.

I could tell within minutes that someone had hours upon hours of work ahead of them, maybe even months.

Wilma, Harry's widow, was certainly not up to it. This is one of the cruel ironies of having a loved one die, the legal and financial systems require a great deal of time and effort from those left behind, involving lots of complicated forms as well as tax and legal technicalities. Some leave behind complex financial issues either because a lot of money is involved…or because a lot of debt is involved.

This left their daughter and co-trustee, Betty, to work it all out. Unfortunately Betty had a full-time job and was not up to the task of taking on another full-time project and this *was* going to be a full-time project. Betty would have to take a full month off work just to sort through the estate.

It surprised me that Harry had left things in such disarray because he knew his time was limited. He had been struggling with his health for months.

He didn't mean to leave his wife such a mystery to unravel. His system made sense to him. He could find anything easily. But to anyone else it was like a jigsaw puzzle but without a picture to guide the assembly.

What could Harry have done differently to save his widow much time and energy?

For starters, he could have consolidated his accounts since there is little benefit to having multiple bank and brokerage accounts. Unless one of the bank accounts went over the FDIC limit, they really only needed one checking account. Multiple brokerage accounts are generally a bad idea. See Chapter Six on 'Diworsification' where I address this topic.

He could have provided passwords if he had them to all the various accounts. Generally a password is required to access accounts online. Often a password is required to access accounts via the telephone as well.

Perhaps most important, he could have left a spreadsheet with all of the following information:

» Title of account
» Contract date (especially for insurance and annuity policies)
» Current Beneficiary information
» Dollar Value, perhaps he could update this annually
» Contract or account number
» Closed accounts with the closing date (this allows heirs to know which accounts are open)

If you want to simplify things for your heirs, leave

this worksheet somewhere it can be found easily.

Perhaps the most important thing you can do is communicate with your heirs, particularly with your partner. I'm an advocate of talking to your spouse about your finances and being completely open. The challenge sometimes is getting them to care, but make the effort.

SUMMARY

Look at your records as if you were seeing them for the first time. Can someone unfamiliar with your affairs sort through them easily? At least annually, update a spreadsheet with some basic information, contract or account numbers, dollar values, date closed, etc. Simplify, simplify, simplify whenever possible.

Chapter 12

YES, I KILLED EVERYONE IN MY CAR... BUT I HAD TO SWERVE TO MISS THE RABBIT

When I was in my early twenties, I loved to ski. Once, driving my friend's car back from a successful ski weekend, a jackrabbit ran onto the highway. We were cruising along at 70 miles per hour, the four of us having a fine time chatting about our adventure, when the rabbit came at us from the slow lane, fangs bared, claws at the ready.

I panicked, slamming on the brakes, wrenching the wheel to the left, and sent the car into a dangerous skid. My passengers were thrown around inside the car and the vehicles behind me had to slam on their brakes to avoid hitting me.

I hit the rabbit anyway.

What did I learn from this experience? I love animals but it did teach me that killing four adults, some of whom were parents, would not be good. It would have been much wiser for me to just grit my teeth and keep driving. Given the choice, I'll save my friends. Goodbye rabbit.

What does this have to do with investing? Simple. If you panic, you will make mistakes.

In January 2009, I was working on some paperwork at my desk when the phone rang. It was Jerry, a relatively new client, and he sounded a bit breathless.

Jerry said, "Kevin, we need to cash out. This market is tanking."

At that point, I heard his wife Lori chime in on the conversation, "Yes, we don't want to lose all of our money!"

"Jerry and Lori, I don't want you to lose all of your money either. But is that really happening?"

I knew that their portfolio wasn't entirely in the stock market and had been designed specifically to cushion the blows of a decline. They had been listening to the news and assumed that their portfolio was moving in lockstep with the market.

"We keep hearing about how bad the market is and are panicking a bit."

Even though I'd talked to Jerry just a few days before,

outlining what was happening with their account, he had clearly forgotten the details. It was apparent that Lori was beyond being merely worried. Her voice was high pitched and strained.

Even though I attempted to soothe their fears and give them a more realistic view of their portfolio, they were determined to jump out.

Jerry and Lori are a couple in their forties. They have two beautiful children in junior high and high school. Jerry is a high income earner while Lori runs the household. Over the years they'd been able to accumulate a sizable balance in their retirement accounts. But the market debacle in the early 2000s was hard on them and even several years later they were still a little skittish.

So when the markets declined in 2008, they decided to cash out and move the bulk of their investments to fixed income investments and there was nothing I could do about it.

In January of 2009, they moved out of the markets. Sure enough, the market, as measured by the S&P 500 continued to decline until early March of 2009, then it reversed course and rocketed up from a closing low of 676 on March 9, 2009 to a closing price of 1,115 on December 31st of 2009, a gain of nearly 65 percent!

Jerry and Lori had the opportunity to regain a very large portion of the losses they had sustained over previous years but they "sold low." What a shame.

It's like watching someone step on a nail in slow motion.

It's especially painful when you consider that they really didn't need the money at the time. In fact, most of their investments were tied up in retirement accounts that they were unable to access without penalty until age 59.5 anyway. They could have left it alone and enjoyed the rebound.

Jerry and Lori panicked and paid a high price for that mistake.

Older investors are also often better served riding out the ups and downs of the market, assuming they've bought appropriate products or implemented investment styles that are suitable for their specific situation.

What should you do when the markets decline? Certainly revisit your strategy. Ask questions, find out whether you should be moving to a more defensive stance or a more aggressive one. Are there alternatives you should be investigating?

Again, if your portfolio was structured properly from the start, odds are you should stick with what you're doing. If you start to modify things every time the market hiccups, you'll continually put yourself in the unenviable position of buying high and selling low, thus defeating the purpose of this exercise.

When do investors panic? Usually they panic when the stock market goes down. Sometimes an investor will place money in the capital markets. Then the markets will decline and they'll panic. Or they'll invest and enjoy a rising market for a while. Then the markets will decline, and they'll panic. Or the markets will go up, and keep going up, until one bad day. It doesn't even have to be a really bad day, just a slightly bad day and they'll panic.

What happens when they panic? Human nature makes us pull out of the markets telling ourselves that we'll 'watch it for a while' before jumping back in.

Let's think this through. The market declines. We get out. This means we are essentially selling low. Now we want to "watch it for a while." What are we looking for? We're looking for the market to go up so we feel comfortable investing again. We watch it go up. Then after the market has enjoyed a rise in value, we jump back in at this new higher value.

That is called selling low and buying high. The stock market is the only market we enter and ignore the sale and discount signs. Instead we deliberately look to buy the stuff that was on sale yesterday, but is back at regular price today.

So what should you consider when the market declines? And how do you know if you're panicking?

After all, most of us will make a decision under pressure but deny that we are panicking.

First off, if you're placed in a position where disaster is looming because of a market decline, it's possible you were invested improperly from the start. By definition, monies we invest need to be left alone for the long term. This is why financial planners nearly always recommend keeping at least three to six months of cash available at all times to cover living expenses. Sometimes more.

Diversification and asset allocation provide no guarantees against market declines, but they do provide some comfort when you realize that you don't have "all your eggs in one basket." If you follow the institutional model I discussed in the chapter "How to Invest Like a Billionaire," you'll ultimately hold dozens, hundreds, maybe even thousands of different securities in your portfolio. While it is possible that they will all decline in value at the same time, it's unlikely. If that were to happen, the world economy would be in such dreadful shape that none of this would really matter, would it?

Finally, think about the times in the past when the stock market went down and never recovered. Can't remember when that happened? Right, because it never has happened. The stock market, while it has experienced significant declines, has recovered every time. Every…single…time. The only question was how long it took. The challenge is whether you can wait for your investments to recover should you be unfortunate enough to hit a flat spot in the markets. A cash reserve can help you solve this issue.

BUYER BEWARE:

Henry and Elizabeth were two investors in their seventies. When the market sustained such significant declines in 2008 and 2009, Henry panicked and moved his money to cash. Elizabeth held her ground, figuring that she had enough cash elsewhere to live on and could allow this investment to work itself out.

In just a few short months, Elizabeth made all of her money back and then some. Henry only had the capital loss to report for tax purposes.

Henry called me sheepishly some time later, expressing his disappointment that he had panicked. He had made the mistake of watching an investment after he sold it. By the way, don't do that, nothing good can come from watching an investment you no longer own.

What should you take away from this chapter?

First, keep enough cash on hand to outlast a market correction. Some planners advise keeping as much as two years cash on hand to allow you as an investor to ride out inevitable market fluctuations.

Second, plan your portfolio from the beginning with a market correction in mind, because it is going to happen; there's no way to avoid it. Your financial advisor, if you use one, should be able to give you an idea of how your portfolio reacted in previous market corrections.

While past performance is no guarantee of future results, we can get some idea of what to expect by looking at how various portfolios acted in past market turmoil. What we're looking for is a portfolio that experienced less volatility than a benchmark we've chosen.

Third, look at products and investment styles that match your risk tolerance. If seeing your portfolio fluctuate keeps you awake at night, makes your stomach turn over, or causes arguments between you and your significant other, you may want to opt for investments that provide lower returns but maintain principal value. On the other hand, perhaps you've done your research and know that the real nemesis is the double barreled threat of inflation and taxes. You may be willing to ride out the ups and downs of investing knowing that this may be your best shot at keeping up with these two adversaries.

Fourth, ask your advisor about the possibility of placing limits on the amount you can lose. Is there a way to place a floor under your investments? Investors will sometimes direct their advisor to get them out when the markets decline a specific amount. For example, they might say, "If the markets decline 20 percent, I want out."

I'm not in favor of this approach for most investors, because it creates a "buy high, sell low" scenario as outlined above. But for some, it meets an emotional need that should be considered.

If you find yourself saying "I want to watch it for a while" before investing, you're probably making a mistake. What are you going to watch it do? Go up? Go down? Go sideways?

If it goes down, will you then invest? No, human nature forces us to refrain from investing when the market is going down. What if it goes down more? We wait for it to go up, then we invest. If it goes sideways, we don't want to invest because we haven't seen any clear direction, so we say "Why invest?" If it goes up, then we say to ourselves, "Ah, the market is going in the right direction, now it's time to invest." Which makes some sort of sense on the surface but what has really happened? We waited until the market went up, lost out on the rise and are buying high.

When then is the best time to invest? When you have money. Implement financial planning principles as highlighted in this book and you will be on the right path toward your goal.

SUMMARY

Consider yourself to be the "Rip Van Winkle" of investing. If Rip had invested, then slept for twenty years, he likely would have woken up, taken a look at his portfolio, and felt that he did pretty well. He wouldn't have known that along the way the markets experienced declines, bear markets, and extended flat spots. He'd only know that he made money. Take the "Rip Van Winkle" approach.

Chapter 13

HOW LONG DO I KEEP DOCUMENTS AND RECORDS?

In our "paperless" society, we are deluged with… paper. Credit card statements, bank statements, brokerage firm statements, the list is endless. What do you do with all those documents? In the chapter on Identity Theft, we discuss the need to shred statements we no longer need. But how do we know when it's time to shred?

There are certain items that we may need to keep a lifetime. For example, when you sell an investment, such as a stock, you must report both the purchase price and the sale price to the Internal Revenue Service on your tax return. How will you know the purchase price if it happened many years ago? You'll need your statement. How will you prove you paid a certain bill? You'll need a canceled check or a copy of it.

There is a flaw in the system. Some statements do

not reflect the purchase price, known as the "cost basis," of stocks, bonds and other investments. Why keep it if it doesn't contain the information you need?

This requires action on your part. The first step is to look at your investment account statement. Does it reflect the cost basis of your investments? If it does not, call your financial advisor and ask him or her to add cost basis information. This should be no problem.

Once you're certain that you have the cost basis reflected on your statement, my advice is to keep your statements throughout the year. When your year-end statement arrives, *then* shred January through November's statements. Keep just your end of year statements and keep them forever.

This changes slightly if you go "paperless." You accomplish this by creating an online user name and password for your brokerage firm and obtaining your statements from its website. This eliminates all the paper statements you may receive in the mail. Your brokerage firm likely allows you to access your statements for many previous years. Note that if you opt for paperless statements, it's still a good idea to print your year-end statements and keep them indefinitely.

But if you have questions about how long to hold on to statements, the list of the following common documents should be helpful.

DOCUMENT	NUMBER OF YEARS TO KEEP
Bank Reconciliations and Bank Statements	Seven
Bank Statements, End of Year	Permanently
Deeds, Mortgages, and Bills of Sale	Permanently
Investment Statements, End of Year	Permanently
Insurance records, accident reports, claims, current policies, etc.	Permanently
Legal and other important Correspondence	Permanently
Stock and Bond Certificates (Canceled)	Seven
Stock and Bond Cost Basis Statements	Permanently
Income Tax Returns and Worksheets	Permanently

This is a conservative approach, and others may tell you differently, but I've seen too many situations where we needed statements from thirty or more years ago but were unable to obtain them, creating a challenge for the investor.

For a more complete listing of documents and how long they should be retained, go to www.makeyourmoneylastalifetime and click on "Resources."

Your final word on this should be your attorney or

tax preparer as there are far more possibilities than we can cover here.

Chapter 14

IDENTITY THEFT

(I BOUGHT 30 PEOPLE DINNER LAST WEEKEND—I WISH I'D BEEN THERE, IT MUST HAVE BEEN FUN)

The young woman behind the counter didn't seem impressed with my explanation. In fact, I'm pretty sure she rolled her eyes at me, a universal code meaning something like "yeah, whatever." I could understand why she'd be frustrated. Twice she had attempted to process my credit card and twice it had been declined.

"Certainly we can call the bank and straighten this out," I said without much hope. After all, I was in Mexico, and there wasn't an 800 number available to call my bank. My cell phone worked in most places, but not at my hotel where I was attempting to rent the car.

"We're not able to do that, sir. What would you like

to do?" she said while peering over my shoulder at the next person in line, as if to indicate that I either needed to figure something out, or she was moving on to the next, presumably paying customer.

Finally, to save face and to get things rolling, I handed her my debit card, something I wouldn't normally do in the United States for a car rental, much less in a Third World country. But what choice did I have? I was certainly going to check with my bank as soon as possible.

Thankfully the debit card charge went through and I was in possession of the keys to one of the smallest cars I'd ever seen, but perfect for our drive.

What had happened? If you're like me, you'd be on the phone the instant the plane landed at home, calling the bank, asking why your credit card, which clearly had plenty of available credit, didn't work. I had even called the bank before leaving the country telling them where I would be so they wouldn't be suspicious of foreign transactions.

The first thing that happened when I called the bank is the on-hold recording gave me the balance of the account, the payment due, and the available credit. There was no available credit. In fact, I was over the limit, so I waited on the line for a live person.

The credit card employee who came on the line

reviewed the last several transactions with me, and come to find out, among other charges I had paid for dinner for a large group of people at Chili's Restaurant in Thousand Oaks, CA. Sadly, I was in Mexico at the day and time that the charge went through, so I apparently missed out on a memorable meal. In fact, the card had been in my wallet the whole time.

I wanted to know, how DO you spend over $600 on a meal at a relatively inexpensive restaurant? Doesn't that send up a red flag? There were other miscellaneous charges on the card, totaling thousands of dollars and exceeding its credit limit.

I was the victim of identity theft. It happens thousands of times every day, around the world, so it shouldn't have come as too much of a surprise. But I've taught classes on identity theft and how to minimize it and knew the steps I needed to take to defend myself.

Seniors are often the victims of identity theft. While identity theft can usually be unraveled, it is a time consuming, laborious, frustrating process and ultimately costs the innocent parties money to correct.

So how can you protect yourself from identity theft? There are three different stages and we want to be familiar with the first two immediately. Then if we become victims of identity theft, we want to learn the third stage promptly, or at least know where to look so that we can clean up the mess.

DETER

The first step in protecting yourself from identity theft is to deter it in the first place. If you can take precautions that deter identity theft, then your chances of having to spend a portion of your life straightening out the mess lessen considerably.

What are the steps to deterring identity theft?

1. Protect your Social Security number. Don't carry your Social Security card with you and don't give it out to just anyone who asks. If someone asks for your Social Security number, ask why they need it and if something else might suffice. Unfortunately, Medicare cards show your Social Security number so guard yours carefully.

2. Be careful with your mail. Never leave mail containing checks out for the mail carrier to pick up. Always take mail containing checks or any personal information directly to the post office.

3. One man's trash is another man's treasure. Never has that been truer than when we're discussing identity theft. What then can you do with your trash to protect yourself? Shred anything that has personally identifiable information, including bank statements, brokerage statements, charge receipts, expired charge cards, insurance forms, physician's statements. Even those

offers you receive for new "Pre-approved" credit cards should be shredded. Why? Because someone could take them from your trash and use them to apply for credit in your good name.

If in doubt as to whether to shred, err on the side of caution. One important caveat: Do NOT shred items that should be saved. Ask your CPA or attorney for help with this.

What type of shredder should you use? Frank Abagnale, whose life story was told in the movie "Catch Me If You Can," is now an FBI employee specializing in identity theft. Frank says to use a "cross cut" shredder which reduces your paper almost to dust.

4. This is obvious but be cautious when using the Internet. Millions of safe, secure transactions occur over the Internet every day so you don't need to avoid the Internet completely but you do need to apply some common sense. For tips on how to use the Internet safely, visit www.OnGuardOnline.gov.

5. Keep your personal information safe and secure in your home. If you share a space with another person, employ outside help, or otherwise have others in your home, it's wise to secure your important papers. Some have a fire-proof safe installed where they can keep important documents. If you do have a safe installed, be certain that it is somewhere easily accessible to you.

6. Don't get careless with your purse or wallet. Today, more than ever, it's important to keep your personal items in sight when dining, going to the movies, shopping and so forth.

7. If the prospect of identity theft really sends chills up your spine, you do have the ability to place a "freeze" on your credit. What is a credit freeze? Each state has its own set of laws but in essence it means that no one can open a new credit account in your name without your specific authorization. You'd need to contact each of the three credit reporting agencies (we'll discuss these agencies in a moment) and perhaps pay them each a fee to implement the freeze. You'll have to call the credit reporting agencies and do a little bit of research to determine the steps to take in your home state.

8. Consider turning off paper statements. Most financial institutions offer customers the option to suspend paper statements and receive statements exclusively online. This option would make sense for you if you're comfortable going online to review your accounts. You could save the time and hassle of shredding all that paper you receive every month.

9. Should you use debit or credit cards? Frank Abagnale, the FBI agent I mentioned earlier, says that he uses a credit card almost exclusively.

Not long ago, I experienced the theft of both my

debit and my credit cards simultaneously and it taught me a powerful lesson. My bank stopped payment on the fraudulent credit transaction, $300 at a Target store in Maryland. The same bank, however, allowed nearly $1,000 in debit card transactions made in Russia. I learned that when they are protecting their money (via a credit card transaction), they won't allow a $300 Target purchase. But when it comes to protecting my money (via a debit card transaction), they allow hundreds of dollars to be charged in some Russian outpost.

As you can guess, I no longer use debit cards for anything.

10. It's a small thing, but using the correct pen when writing checks can make a difference. You've heard the term "check washing." Check washing is when the bad guys get their hands on a check you've written then place tape over your signature, front and back, to protect it during the check washing process. They then soak the check in a solution that removes all of your writing from the check. When the check dries, they remove the tape that protected your signature and they're left with a signed, blank check which they can then make out to any party they choose for any amount they choose.

How to protect yourself from check washing? Frank Abagnale developed a pen with a special ink that thieves cannot wash off. It's called the Uniball 207 and can be found at almost any office supply store. I use a Uniball 207 exclusively when writing checks.

DETECT

The next step in minimizing damage from identity theft is to detect it when it happens, and this requires ongoing vigilance on your part. You're going to need to read your bank, credit card, and brokerage statements carefully as soon as they arrive in the mail. Look for transactions you don't recognize.

Again, I like to turn off paper statements completely and only view my accounts online. This way, no one can steal paper statements from my mailbox or trash.

Review your own credit report three times per year. Each credit reporting agency, Experian, Equifax, and Transunion must provide you with one credit report annually. So set a schedule for yourself and take advantage of this free service. They will attempt to sell you services while you're visiting their sites—after all, they are in business to make money—but you can obtain your credit report for free.

When reviewing your credit report, look for accounts you don't recognize, past due amounts, incorrect addresses, anything that doesn't look quite right. Even an employer that might be listed on your employment history that you didn't work for could be a potential identity theft in the making.

We need to be aware on a daily basis since unexplained and mysterious events can indicate that someone is messing with your identity. Here are some things you should be on the watch for:

Receiving a phone call regarding a transaction that docsn't sound familiar. One friend of mine received a phone call from a furniture company that was attempting to deliver furniture but had gotten lost. Someone had stolen their identity, opened a charge account in their name, purchased furniture, and asked for it to be delivered to the thief's house. The delivery truck got lost, obtained my friend's phone number through 411, and called her to ask for directions.

This was the clue that led my friend to uncover identity theft. A total fluke but it does illustrate that we need to be on guard. If something odd happens, don't just ignore it. It just may be a tip-off that your identity has been stolen.

Receiving a statement in the mail from a company that you don't recognize, such as a credit card company, could indicate that someone has established an account in your name.

Alternatively, not receiving mail from your financial services companies should set off alarm bells in your head. Why? Because if someone were to change the address on your account and divert your mail, then place charges on your account, how long might it be before you found out? Keep track of approximately when your credit card, bank and other statements usually arrive. If they're ever late by a week or so, call the company and ask for a copy. While you have them on the phone, be sure to ask what address they have on file, and inquire about recent charges and current balance while you're at it.

Receiving a call from a bill collector regarding a debt you're not aware of could be a signal that someone has opened an account in your name.

Being denied credit unexpectedly, or being charged a higher than normal interest rate because of your "risky" credit rating should be a wake-up call. You need to find out what the creditor is basing their decision on. Is there something on your credit report that you are unaware of?

The place to go to gain access to your free report every four months is www.annualcreditreport.com and only www.annualcreditreport.com. The many sites that sound similar to this site are bogus and should be avoided.

You may decide to pay a fee to a company that will monitor your credit report and alert you whenever someone attempts to access your credit. There are many choices out there, so just be sure you understand what you're paying for before committing to any particular service.

BUYER BEWARE:

Ted was enjoying a relaxing day at home when the phone rang. Expecting one of his children, or perhaps even one of his many grandchildren to be on the line, he answered in a lighthearted manner. His change in manner told his wife, Sally, that the call wasn't pleasant, not pleasant at all.

"'This is Sergeant Matthews with the Police Department. Is this Ted Wilson?"

Ted is in his sixties and nobody's fool, so he played this very carefully.

"This is Ted, what's up?"

"Sir, we believe that you've been the victim of identity theft. In a recent drug bust, we found checks made out in your name and we need to confirm some information with you."

RED FLAG! Ted, being a smart guy, knew that he had to watch his step here. What if this was really a fraudster hoping to get Ted to reveal some personal information?

"I tell you what, give me your name again and I'll call you."

The man on the other end of the line gave his name and rank with the police department, told Ted which police station he worked from and Ted promptly hung up. Now all Ted had to do was look up the police station's phone number and call in, ask for this police sergeant and he would know whether the call was legitimate.

Very smart move on his part, wouldn't you say? And a good lesson for all of us to remember. Ted was somewhat surprised when he called the Police Department from the number listed in the phone book, asked for the sergeant who had supposedly called him, the sergeant answered, and…it was the same guy! This call really was from the Police Department.

At this point, Ted had mixed feelings. He was glad that the call hadn't come from someone trying to commit fraud, but it also meant that he probably was the victim of identity theft as the officer had told him at the start.

"Sir, first off I wanted to thank you for taking the precaution of calling me back. That means you're conscious of the threat of identity theft. You have no idea how many people start telling me personal information over the phone with no basis for knowing whether I'm really a police officer or not.

To them, I'm just a voice on the other end of the line but I'm often given very personal information by complete strangers. It's disturbing, to be honest."

"Tell me what's up," Ted asked. He was anxious to learn what was going on, why the police were calling him and how concerned he should be.

The story he was told was bizarre, full of coincidence and disturbing. The police had been tracking a young woman for months who was on parole from prison for drug charges and had been living in a trailer. The police had carefully collected evidence for some time, initiated because she was suspected of again dealing drugs. Finally, feeling that they had sufficient reason to raid her home, they did just that and found a large cache of drugs.

How did this concern Ted? Was he somehow mixed up in the drug trade? No, but in the process of searching her home, they found a packet of checks with his name and address but with the name of a bank other than the bank he used for his personal banking.

But what made this really interesting was that, while the bank name on the checks was different than the bank Ted used, the ABA number (the number used at the bottom of checks to identify the bank) and the account number on the bottom of the checks were his actual ABA and account numbers. So when the checks were cleared through the banking system, the money would have come out of his account. While Ted didn't experience any actual loss, he came "damn close" as he told me.

It's a sad truth that you can take all of these steps to deter identity theft, you can keep on the lookout for it, you can be careful with your wallet and Social Security number, and keep everything in a safe, and *still* be the victim of identity theft. So what do you do when you realize that your identity has been stolen? Or you even have a strong suspicion?

If you believe your identity may have been stolen, what is your first step? Contact the bank, brokerage firm, or credit card company immediately! Minutes count. In some cases, you will lose your legal protection if not reported within days.

There are four more steps you must take immediately, and they are:

1. Place a fraud alert on your credit report. The good news is that you only have to place the alert with one credit reporting agency, they are then obligated to notify the other two.

Here are the numbers for the three credit reporting agencies:

EXPERIAN (888) 397-3742
EQUIFAX (800) 525-6285
TRANSUNION (800) 680-7289

Once you place a fraud alert on your file, ask for your free credit report which they are obligated to provide once you file a fraud claim.

When you receive your credit report, check it for accuracy. There are the obvious things like accounts you didn't open, balances you shouldn't have, companies you don't recognize. Then there are the less obvious items which you might be inclined to skip, like your address. Is it correct? Are there any employers listed that are inaccurate? What about something as basic as your Social Security number—is it accurate? Identity thieves employ all sorts of sly devices to steal your good reputation.

From the very beginning keep track of anyone you speak to about this issue. Write down the name of the person you spoke with, their employer's name, the phone number you dialed to contact them, the day and time you spoke to them, and what was said.

2. Close any accounts you have reason to believe may have been compromised. Or perhaps there are accounts you don't recognize at all.

Existing accounts that have been compromised should be handled as follows:

Call each company and ask them what form you

need to dispute what you believe is a fraudulent account or charge. Then notify the company in writing about the account in question, informing them you did not place the charges in question on the account and believe that those are fraudulent. Send all letters via certified mail with return receipt requested. You want to be able to prove that you notified the creditor and when they were notified. Keep track of all of your correspondence and conversations with them.

Once you have resolved the matter with the company, ask for a letter from them stating that the matter has been handled and the fraudulent account has been closed. You never know when you might need proof of this in the future.

3. File a formal complaint with the Federal Trade Commission. You and others will benefit from this. You will benefit because when you file with the FTC, you can print a copy of your online complaint form and provide that to the police. When combined with the police report, you have an "Identity Theft Report" and an extra layer of protection. Now you can permanently block this fraudulent information from appearing on your credit report. You can ensure that these debts don't reappear on your report, you can prevent a company from continuing to call to collect these debts and you can place an extended fraud alert on your credit report.

4. If you haven't already, file a police report.

Surprisingly, some police officers may not be aware that you can report identity theft just like any other theft. They may be inexperienced, or just unaware. Don't let that deter you. The ideal option is to go to the police station with a printed copy of your FTC complaint form along with a cover letter.

This cover letter is taken from the Federal Trade Commission's website, and is directed to law enforcement so that the police officer will understand why their report, combined with the FTC paperwork, is so important. The FTC website says to "Ask the officer to attach or incorporate the ID Theft Complaint into their police report. Tell them that you need a copy of the Identity Theft Report (the police report with your ID Theft Complaint attached or incorporated) to dispute the fraudulent accounts and debts created by the identity thief."

The police are not obligated to incorporate the FTC form in your identity theft report, but either way, the report they provide is called an Identity Theft Report (mentioned above) and should be submitted to the credit reporting agencies.

When you go back to the credit reporting agencies, ask what other steps you should take in addition to submitting the Identity Theft Report, in order to protect your good credit.

For more valuable information on how to protect yourself from identity theft, go to www.makeyourmoneylastalifetime and click on "Resources."

SUMMARY

Identity theft is expensive and time consuming so be alert!

Deter identity theft by safeguarding your personally identifiable information.

Shred documents.

Don't give your information to anyone who calls you on the phone.

Be skeptical.

Detect identity theft by carefully reading your financial statements as soon as you receive them. If something odd happens, for example you receive a statement you don't recognize or get a phone call regarding a purchase you didn't make, don't ignore it! It might be a clue that your identity has been stolen or compromised.

Defend against identity theft by reporting anything odd immediately! Minutes count!

Chapter 15

SCAMS!

Vic held the phone close to his ear and listened carefully as the caller sobbed, "Grandpa, I need help!" Vic could barely understand the words spoken through the tears. The caller went on, "I…I…" but the words were choked off as he took a breath.

"Who is this? Johnny? Is that you?" Vic's only grandson, Johnny, lived nearby with his parents in Santa Barbara, California.

The voice on the phone replied, "Yes, grandpa, it's Johnny. I did something stupid. Please don't tell my folks. They'd kill me!"

"Ok, slow down, slow down. Tell me what happened." And with those words, Vic was hooked.

Vic is in his early seventies, married, with two sons. His older son, Michael, has two children, a boy and a girl, both teenagers. Michael's son is named John.

They've called Michael's son 'Johnny,' since the day he was born.

Through the tears, Johnny went on to explain that he had been instructed by his parents not to go out with his friends in Las Vegas where he was visiting. Instead of listening he had gone out with a group of teenagers. One of them had been drinking and driving, they'd been in an accident, and now Johnny was in jail needing cash for bail.

All Vic needed to do was send money via Western Union to pay the bail and get him out. Three thousand dollars would cover it.

Vic faced a dilemma. Call the parents? Or not? While many would automatically involve the parents, that isn't true of all grandparents. Some would choose to help their grandchildren get out of this jam. Under stress, we all do unexpected things.

Johnny pushed hard for Vic to send money as soon as possible so that he could get out of the Vegas jail. But Vic wasn't quite sure he shouldn't get his son Michael involved. Vic felt he should talk to Michael first.

He told Johnny he would call him back, but of course Johnny didn't have a phone number to give Vic. Johnny said that he would call back in ten minutes, and that he had to go because some thug in the jail wanted to use the phone and was threatening him. Then Johnny hung up. Vic didn't even get to ask where to find Johnny if he needed him.

By now Vic was panicking so he called his son Michael.

"Michael, how is your day going?" Vic aimed to direct the conversation around to Johnny to see what he could learn. And he wanted to know as quickly as possible.

Michael told his Dad that he was enjoying a glorious sunny day packed with fun activities with his family.

"And what is Johnny up to today?" Vic asked.

"Johnny? Oh, he's outside loading the bicycles on the back of the truck." Michael said breezily. But how could that be? Vic had just heard from Johnny himself in Las Vegas.

Vic tried to sound nonchalant as he asked, "Really, I thought he was out of town?"

"What? Johnny? No, I just sent him out to get the gear ready five minutes ago."

It took Vic a few seconds to process this piece of information. How could Johnny be at home in Santa Barbara, when he had just received the phone call from Las Vegas? Then the truth hit him forcefully and Vic got angry. Angry with the con artist and angry with himself for buying into the story he had been told.

Vic had just finished breakfast when "Johnny" called that morning. He certainly hadn't been expecting to be the prey in a con game.

Would Johnny call back? Sure enough, within just a few minutes of Vic hanging up with his son Michael, the phone rang. "Johnny" was calling back as promised. This time Vic was determined to "give him a piece of his mind" but "Johnny" hung up the instant he heard the tone in Vic's voice.

So many of my clients have been approached over the years with this particular scam that I believe there must be thousands of crooks trying the same thing across the United States all day long. A con artist can sit down with a phone book and dial numbers all day long telling the same story over and over, faking the sobbing and collecting an untold amount of cash.

How many dozens of innocent people can a thief call in the course of a day? And how many need to fall for the scam for the thief to collect thousands of dollars in a day?

In Vic's case, the caller asked for $3,000. Transferred electronically… untraceable …disappearing into thin air.

It's shocking how much money a thief can make tax free, sitting in the comfort of his or her own living room talking on the phone.

BUYER BEWARE:

Suzanne thought she'd found a great deal online

from her favorite department store and ordered a piece of jewelry for a quarter of its normal price. She told her friends over breakfast, then again at lunch, about the great deal she had found. For two weeks she looked forward to receiving her jewelry.

When it did finally arrive, it was obvious that this wasn't the high-quality item she expected but rather a cheap imitation, clearly not the item she would have received had she walked into the store.

Suzanne complained to the department store but learned that the site she had ordered from wasn't the store's site but rather another site that looked similar. In the end she learned that her product was inferior but there was nothing she could do.

Have you been scammed by a con artist?

There are innumerable cons out there, and new ones are concocted every day. If you're a retiree, you need to be especially on guard. Unfortunately, you are a prime target for con artists.

Have you received a phone call, letter or email informing you that you can purchase prescription drugs at a discount price? Maybe you're told that for a small entry fee, you'll receive a much larger prize from a sweepstakes.

In the case of one man, he received numerous letters telling him that he had won a large prize and all he needed to do was send in twenty dollars to claim it. Once he accepted an offer like this, his mailbox was flooded with similar offers. Unfortunately he responded to dozens before a friend alerted him to the fact that all of these were fake offers, simply designed to collect money from him.

Often e-mails supposedly from large banks, maybe even the bank you use for your checking or savings, are bogus. They appear to be from your bank but they're really from someone fishing for information. This practice of sending illegitimate e-mails with the intent to collect personal information is actually called "phishing."

There is not enough space here to list all of the various scams thieves use to steal money from innocent people but retirees are often special targets and so need to be aware. Unsolicited phone calls, strangers at the door, that nice person you met at the grocery store, the young person from the charity that knocks on your door, insurance products that seem too good to be true, there are thousands of variations played out by con artists.

The old sayings "you can't be too careful," and "if it seems too good to be true," have never been more accurate. I urge you to use extreme caution when giving money to anyone or any organization that is new to your life. If in doubt, ask someone you trust, your children, your financial advisor, your tax preparer, your attorney.

SUMMARY

Scams are prolific and new ones sprout every day.
Use extreme caution when money is involved.
Ask someone you trust for help.
Be skeptical.

Chapter 16

IN CONCLUSION...

Here's a letter we received recently:

"Dear Kevin,

THOUGHTS ON FINANCIAL SECURITY
FOR WOMEN OVER 60

The biggest surprise is when, all of a sudden, you're 60 and you really don't have any financial security. Or at least you THINK you don't.

After years of believing I never would be able to depend on Social Security (a system that has supposedly been broken for so long that even in my forties I never thought I'd see the day when I actually received it), I realize that I will be very dependent on it.

Another surprise is the idea of working until age 70. When I was growing up, people retired at 65 and died a couple of years later. Sixty was OLD. Now we have a good chance of living until we're 90. So, working until 70—and actually feeling quite young at 62—is a good thing!

Another upside is that by waiting until 70 to take Social Security, it will be nearly double the amount I could get at my "full retirement age" of 66. And, because of large investment losses in my late 50s (in particular the dot com bust and then the current recession), I will need every bit of the next eight years to build up as much as I can in terms of Social Security credits and investments in order to spin off enough to live on in retirement.

I likely will choose to work part time in "retirement" anyway, because I want to and it's healthier, based on a lot of research done on what happens when you "fall off the working cliff" and just stop. I look forward to working in places that interest me, such as nurseries and bookstores.

My biggest concern is that I know I won't be able to continue the mortgage payments on my home when I stop working full time and I cannot pay off the mortgage before that happens. So, the plan is to make some money on it, cash out and live someplace I can afford. It's heartbreaking after a full and active life to think I won't be able to own my home in retirement. But that's how it's looking.

One of the most important things I can advise is having a financial advisor. Finding the right one is critical. One I had along the way allowed me to lose everything, including my initial investment, in the dot com bust. Another after that left his company and never bothered telling me."

It was hearing such legitimate concerns that drove me to write this book. Finances, for many, are in a black box that seems impenetrable. Money can be mysterious, difficult to manage, difficult to understand, and difficult to hold on to.

While investment management is at the core of your finances, there are many false steps that can destroy even the best portfolio management. Ignoring the level of risk you're taking can be harmful to your financial health. Too little risk and inflation and taxes eat up your nest-egg. Too much risk and you might end up going back to work in your later years just to make ends meet.

Giving too much to the kids too soon can be harmful. As can hiring the wrong advisor. Not updating your beneficiary statements can wreak havoc on your heirs. Keeping your employer's stock after retiring can be devastating.

All these items may seem minor in comparison to actual investment management, but in the end, may be even more important to you—and your heirs'—financial well-being.

There are many websites that I use often that may be useful to you as well:

Internal Revenue Service: WWW.IRS.GOV

FDIC: WWW.FDIC.GOV

SIPC: WWW.SIPC.ORG

Social Security Administration: WWW.SSA.GOV

Federal Trade Commission: WWW.FTC.GOV

Medicare: WWW.MEDICARE.GOV

I hope this book has gotten you thinking about questions you should be asking. If so, it will have served its purpose.

Follow the steps you've read here, and move ahead with confidence.

ABOUT THE AUTHOR

Kevin Bourke, CERTIFIED FINANCIAL PLANNER ™ Professional, CHARTERED FINANCIAL CONSULTANT and CERTIFIED DIVORCE FINANCIAL ANALYST, started his career in 1987. Since that time he's been helping investors make wise financial decisions, especially when they were faced with major life transitions.

Kevin has been a financial columnist for the Santa Barbara Independent and is regularly featured on KEYT/ABC News. As a public speaker, he has helped thousands of listeners become smarter with their money.

He believes that much care and attention is necessary when managing investments and feels that a good financial advisor must go beyond portfolio management and assist in making wise decisions regarding taxes, insurance, education, estate planning and more.

Kevin lives in lovely Santa Barbara, CA. His stated goal is to help one million retirees, seniors and their adult children become smarter with their money.

In looking to the future, he feels investors will need to be increasingly fee conscious, more aware of investment risk, better educated on global issues and ever-more patient.

Kevin has two daughters who remind him daily of what's really important.

KEVIN CAN BE REACHED AT:

Kevin Bourke
Bourke Wealth Management
1032 Santa Barbara Street
Santa Barbara, CA 93101
Telephone: 805.966.2122
Email: kevin.bourke@lpl.com

CPSIA information can be obtained at www.ICGtesting.com
Printed in the USA
LVOW08s1552300913

354763LV00001B/74/P